THE UNION
IS DISSOLVED!

THE UNION IS DISSOLVED!

CHARLESTON AND FORT SUMTER IN THE CIVIL WAR

DOUGLAS W. BOSTICK

Charleston · London

THE
History
PRESS

Published by The History Press
Charleston, SC 29403
www.historypress.net

All images are from the author's collection unless otherwise noted.

First published 2009
Second printing 2011
Third printing 2013

Manufactured in the United States

ISBN 978.1.59629.573.5

Library of Congress Cataloging-in-Publication Data

Bostick, Douglas W.
The Union is dissolved! : Charleston and Fort Sumter in the Civil War / Douglas W.
Bostick.
p. cm.
Includes bibliographical references.
ISBN 978-1-59629-573-5
1. Charleston (S.C.)--History--Civil War, 1861-1865. 2. Fort Sumter (Charleston,
S.C.)--Siege, 1861. 3. Secession--Southern States. 4. United States--History--Civil War,
1861-1865--Causes. I. Title.
E471.1.B67 2009
973.7--dc22
2009023234

This book is dedicated to my dear friend,
Brigadier General Hugh B. Tant III.
He has always conducted himself understanding the greatest calling for any
citizen—that of being a Patriot. His only motivation in his illustrious career
was to serve his country and his fellow man with honor and integrity. The
great spirit of our South Carolina forefathers is exemplified in his conduct, his
devotion to duty and his life.

CONTENTS

ACKNOWLEDGEMENTS

I was raised in the shadow of Fort Sumter. As a kid, my friends and I would ride bicycles to Fort Johnson and gaze out to the harbor onto Fort Sumter. We imagined that we were standing next to the beach battery that fired the first shot. We looked back to the city of Charleston, thinking about the crowds assembled at the Battery to watch the spectacle of war. At low tide, we would walk out from Fort Johnson to Fort Sumter collecting artifacts from the war left behind by the tides.

Visiting our local raconteur, Willie McLeod, at his plantation, he taught us that the proper name for the conflict was the War Between the States. He would often remark that calling it the Civil War implied that states were fighting for control of the country. He would remind us that we (the South) did not want control, we just wanted out!

Though this is my tenth book, it is the first book I ever intended to write. I trust that I have been able to humanize the story of the beginning of the war. War is not romantic—war is no fairy tale. Unfortunately, it is the manner in which we seem to resolve our conflicts.

I am indebted to William Ellis McLeod and my grandfather, J. Frank Taylor, for my early education about "the war." In college, I was privileged to take my courses (the American Civil War and the history of the South) from a Citadel professor, Captain Cousins, who would cross town on occasion to teach College of Charleston students about the stories of history he held so dear.

I am indebted to the staff at the Charleston Library Society and the South Carolina Room of the Charleston County Library. Their important collections serve writers and historians well.

Thank you to Laura All, Marshall Hudson and all the staff at The History Press for bringing this important story to print.

ACKNOWLEDGEMENTS

Thank you to my wife Karen and my children, Katey, Brooks and Taylor. They have been most tolerant of my fascination with history and writing. They have inspired me to reach out to tell the great stories of our young country.

It is my hope that this modest history will bring readers to want to know more about the fascinating people who played a role in this American drama. Their lives are worthy of study. Their stories deserve to be told.

CHAPTER 1

THE PRINCIPLES OF SELF-DETERMINATION

S ecession is not a concept of the nineteenth century. The use of force to hold a political union is almost as old as man himself. Interestingly, almost all the attempts to secede have met with failure, in many cases, with disastrous results.

In the fourth century BC, the city-states of Melos and Mytilene attempted to secede from the Athenian League. The revolt was over heavy taxes imposed by Athens. The revolt was put to bed by a brutal war, which proved a lesson to the other city-states. Later, Rome dealt with many attempts through its history of rule.

In the modern era, the Dutch revolt against the Spanish empire initiated sixty years of war. The struggle of Scotland to gain independence from England foreshadowed the events in America centuries later. The Scots battled for five hundred years and finally ended with the Act of Union in 1707. The Disarming Act of 1756 revoked the Scots' right to bear arms. It also banned the use of bagpipes and the wearing of tartans. The Scottish quest for independence can be traced back to 1297–1320 and the Declaration of Arbroath, which stated:

> So long as there shall be but one hundred of us to remain alive we will never give consent to subject ourselves to the dominion of the English. For it is not glory, it is not riches, neither is it honor, but it is freedom alone that we fight and contend for, which no honest man will lose but with his life.

One British officer, known as "Butcher Cumberland," laid waste to the Scottish Highlands, not unlike the march of Sherman to the sea in Georgia.

Of course, another long-standing story of independence is the struggle of Ireland. The battle for Irish secession has lasted for almost four hundred years and is still not fully resolved.

The great irony, of course, of the furor over the secession movement in America is that the creation of the very government that fought to prevent secession was born of secession. That fact was not lost on the British when the North–South conflict emerged in America. "The right of a people by popular consent to secede from a larger nation or confederation when the people believed it no longer served their needs and interests" is the story of the American Revolution. One British scholar wrote, "It is startling to realize that Lincoln did not believe in the principle of self-determination of peoples...Lincoln fought against them with more determination than any British Prime Minister fought against Ireland."

The idea of secession was born in America, though, long before 1860. Massachusetts threatened to secede four times in the history of the young country: over state debts after the Revolution, after the Louisiana Purchase by Jefferson, during the War of 1812 and finally on the annexation of Texas. Unlike Lincoln, Jefferson acknowledged the right of secession if that was the will of Massachusetts.

When ratifying the United States Constitution, Rhode Island, New York and Virginia all retained the right to leave the United States if needed. The Virginia Act, approved on June 26, 1788, stated: "In their name and on behalf of the people of Virginia, declare and make known, that the powers granted under the Constitution, being derived from the people of the United States, may be resumed by them, whenever the same shall be perverted to their injury or oppression."

As a result of the War of 1812, delegates from Massachusetts, Connecticut, Rhode Island, Vermont and New Hampshire met in the Hartford Convention of 1814 to discuss secession. They wanted to change the Constitution to improve states' rights. However, the war ended soon and the movement by the Federalist Party faded.

CHAPTER 2

THE FATHERS OF SECESSION

Thomas Cooper was born in 1759 in Westminster, England. His early life was one of privilege. He attended but dropped out of Oxford University and married while still a teenager. Still, he continued his studies of law and medicine. After a bitter experience in British politics, he left England for America in 1793.

He first settled in Pennsylvania and was an outspoken critic of President John Adams. He taught at Carlisle College and the University of Pennsylvania before accepting a teaching position at South Carolina College in 1819. In 1821, Cooper was elected as the second president of the College, a position he would hold for twelve years.

Active in politics, Cooper took particular exception to protective tariffs. In a speech in Columbia, he insisted, "If he [Northern manufacturers] cannot make goods as cheap and as of good quality, is that a reason why his deficiencies should be made good out of our pocket, by compelling us to pay exorbitant prices?" He asserted that Congress had the right to regulate commerce but had no right to legislate protective tariffs.

He concluded the speech by saying:

> *I have said, that we shall ere long be compelled to calculate the value of our union; and to inquire of what use to us is this most unequal alliance? By which the South has always been the loser and the North always the gainer? Is it worth our while to continue this union of states, where the North demand to be our masters and we are required to be their tributaries? Who with the most insulting mockery call the yoke they put upon our necks the AMERICAN SYSTEM! The question is however fast approaching to the alternative, of submission or separation.*

The secession movement thus began in Columbia, South Carolina, in the 1820s.

THE UNION IS DISSOLVED!

Despite Cooper's pontifications and many protests, Congress, in 1828, passed what was called the Tariff of Abominations. Even though import duties were increased to 50 percent, total tax revenue decreased, as people ceased buying foreign goods. Cooper's writings and speeches had a marked impact on two men: Robert Barnwell Rhett, a young state legislator from Walterboro, and John C. Calhoun, the vice president of the United States in 1828.

The 1828 tariff act forever changed Calhoun's political views. In an essay entitled "The South Carolina Exposition and Protest," Calhoun asserted that states could address their issues with the federal government through nullification, essentially saying that individual states could nullify actions of the government that they deemed unconstitutional.

Though Calhoun was seen previously as a strong "nationalist," politicians now screamed that he was a "sectionalist." A good friend and founder of the Charleston *Mercury*, Henry Pinckney, countered that he and Calhoun were not sectionalists, writing, "We have only changed from being friendly to a system we once imagined would be 'national,' to the opponents of a system which we are now convinced is 'sectional' and 'corrupt.'" Across South Carolina, citizens formed State Rights and Free Trade Associations.

Rhett was a disciple of the writings of Cooper and an ardent supporter of Calhoun. In an Independence Day speech in 1832, Rhett argued, "What sir,

Robert Barnwell Rhett was referred to by some as the "Father of Secession." *Courtesy of the Library of Congress.*

South Carolinian John C. Calhoun wrote the theory of nullification. *Courtesy of the Library of Congress.*

has the people ever gained, but by Revolution?...What sir, Carolina has ever obtained great or free, but by Revolution?...Revolution! Sir, it is the dearest and holiest word, to the brave and free."

On November 24, 1832, delegates to a South Carolina Convention declared the Tariff Acts of 1828 and 1832 to be "null" and "void." It was announced that, effective February 1, 1833, federal duties would no longer be collected in South Carolina.

President Jackson immediately responded by reinforcing the federal garrisons at Fort Moultrie and Castle Pinckney. General Winfield Scott was placed in command and Jackson shipped five thousand muskets to the arsenal at South Carolina. Jackson was quoted as saying, "We shall cross the mountains into...South Carolina with a force, which joined by Union men of that State, will be so overwhelming as to render resistance hopeless."

Calhoun resigned as vice president but continued in Washington as a senator from South Carolina. Rumors were that Jackson had decided to arrest Calhoun for treason. On December 10, 1832, Jackson issued the Proclamation to the People of South Carolina and reiterated his views on federal rule. Additionally, Jackson sent a bill to Congress to force the collection of tariffs in South Carolina.

The Union Is Dissolved!

As the Senate considered the bill, the Calhoun–Daniel Webster debates were most heated. When the bill came up for a vote, all Southern senators, with the exception of John Tyler, walked out of the chamber in protest.

South Carolina began preparations for a federal invasion. The General Assembly voted to spend $400,000 for defense and authorized the governor to call out the militia. On December 26, Governor Robert Hayne issued a call for volunteers and twenty-five thousand men stepped forward. Everyone on both sides was making final preparations for war.

In Washington, Henry Clay and Calhoun were holding secret meetings seeking a resolution. The meetings produced a compromise tariff bill that both men could support. The new bill provided that tariffs would be reduced in steps over nine years. Calhoun was pleased with the outcome. South Carolina had declared a bill to be "null" and "void" and the bill was replaced.

More radical politicians, like Cooper, wanted to continue resisting Jackson, but Calhoun and Rhett favored the compromise. Rhett did, however, agree that he would be happier with the formation of a Southern Confederacy. Knowing that nothing was permanently resolved and recognizing that the principle of protectionism was still intact, he knew that the fight would simply continue.

CHAPTER 3

LINCOLN IS ELECTED

The issues of states' rights and protective tariffs never did fade after the 1830s. The South understood that its political influence was receding as more states were admitted to the Union. The expansion of slavery in the western territories was a central issue. The South wanted slavery to be assured in these new territories, but Northerners wanted the new territories and states to be able to decide the issue for themselves. The Southern states were looking for political support from like-minded states in Congress.

In the frequent debates in the Senate over the issue of slavery expansion, Stephen Douglas argued, "I tell you, gentlemen of the South, in all candor, I do not believe a Democratic candidate can ever carry any one Democratic state of the North on the platform that it is the duty of the Federal Government to force people of a territory to have slavery if they do not want it."

By 1860, cotton was the leading export commodity of the nation. Southern raw goods and agricultural products were much sought after by Northern manufacturers and European interests. The South wanted to trade with Europe, but the protectionist tariffs made European products cost prohibitive. Northern politicians were using the trade tariffs to control Southern raw goods for their own use rather than letting them reach Europe. In short, the Southern states felt that they were being exploited by the Northern majority in Congress.

Author Charles Dickens closely followed the sectional conflict in America and often wrote of the growing tension. In one editorial, he wrote,

> *The North having gradually got to itself the making of the laws and the settlement of the Tariffs, and having taxed the South most abominably for its own advantage, began to see, as the country grew, that unless it advocated*

the laying down of a geographical line beyond which slavery should not extend, the South would necessarily recover its old political power, and be able to help itself a little in the adjustment of commercial affairs.

With the growing tension in the country, a Southern city was selected for the upcoming Democratic Convention in hopes that the setting may bring some unity to the party. *Harper's Weekly* wrote of Charleston:

It [Charleston] *is, we need hardly add, one of the oldest, noblest, and most beautiful cities of the South...As you enter from the sea, between the Islands of Sullivan and Morris, the city opens before you in the foreground, five miles distant—rising, like another Venice, from the ocean.*

One writer compared Charleston to another historic city on the eastern seaboard:

Like Boston, at once its polar opposite and its nearest kin, Charleston was an odd blend of ancestor worship, stifling custom, and practicality. The difference, said one wag, was that a Boston gentleman looked as if he knew everything while a Charlestonian looked as if he knew everything worthwhile for a gentleman to know. The great families of both cities cherished the Revolution as the defining moment in their history, the

Harper's Weekly published this bird's-eye view of Charleston in 1857, referring to the city as "rising, like another Venice, from the ocean."

Downtown Charleston, as depicted in the *Illustrated London News*.

Slave women selling sweet potatoes on the streets of Charleston.

The 1860 National Democratic Party Convention was held at South Carolina Institute Hall at 134 Meeting Street in Charleston.

This engraving of convention delegates was published in *Harper's Weekly*, describing the proceedings as "momentous…and upon the fruit of whose labors the destiny of the Union may depend."

morality play that produced the heroes and lessons they treasured the most. They revered its iconography even as they tightened their own hold over the city and the state. In 1860, a mere 155 of its 40,500 people owned half of Charleston's wealth.

The convention was held at South Carolina Institute Hall. There were a total of 606 delegates, but 3,000 people crowded into the hall to watch the proceedings. The city lacked sufficient hotel rooms and boardinghouses to accommodate the large crowd visiting the city. Even though the convention opened on April 23, visitors began to arrive in town as early as April 18.

Southerners feared that the election of a Republican to the White House was a precursor to the adoption of high-tariff policies. The confluence of these divisive issues contributed to the growing movement for Southern nationalism. Despite the party's conciliatory move to hold the convention in the South, the proceedings and the resulting deadlock proved a fiasco.

Delegates from New England chartered a steamship, the *S.R. Spaulding*, for eighteen days for $10,000 to make the trip to Charleston and for housing on

The Union Is Dissolved!

The city was so overwhelmed by the throngs of delegates and curiosity seekers that the Boston delegates had to stay aboard their steamship, the *S.R. Spaulding*. The large ship carried three brass guns, two of which were used at the Battle of Bunker Hill.

board at the dock during the convention. *Harper's Weekly* noted in an article that the delegates, including the convention chairman, Caleb Cushing, lived on the ship "more cheaply, and probably more comfortable, and certainly more healthily, than in the over-crowded hotels of Charleston."

The delegates spread across the city for housing, choosing to room with other delegates of a similar mind. Delegates supporting Douglas stayed at the Hibernian Hall, which converted its large ballrooms to dormitory-style accommodations. The Buchanan delegates stayed at hotels on King Street, and the delegates favoring secession stayed at the Charleston Hotel.

The factions, divided North and South, remained deadlocked during the convention. The Southern delegates wanted the unconditional protection for slavery in the western territories. The Northern delegates were willing to concede the institution of slavery but wanted each territory to have the right to adopt slavery or abolish it. Slavery was the single dividing issue between Northern and Southern delegates.

Both factions wanted to promote the transcontinental railroad to the Pacific. Both were in favor of the acquisition of Cuba. Both groups opposed the efforts of some states to circumvent the Fugitive Slave Law. Ultimately, the Southern delegates could not support Stephen Douglas with his stance on popular sovereignty.

The Southern delegates proposed a platform plank on the slavery issue that stated:

Charleston and Fort Sumter in the Civil War

The "Douglas" delegates were housed at Hibernian Hall, home of Charleston's Irish Society, depicted in this *Harper's Weekly* engraving.

Resolved, that the Democracy of the United States hold these cardinal principles on the subject of slavery in the Territories: First, that Congress has no power to abolish slavery in the Territories. Second, that the Territorial Legislature has no power to abolish slavery in any Territory, not to prohibit the introduction of slaves therein, nor any power to exclude slavery therefrom, nor any right to destroy or impair the right of property in slaves by any legislation whatever.

On April 30, the proposal was defeated 165–138. The 51 Southern delegates then walked out of the convention. As the Southern delegates left the Institute Hall in protest, they gathered at the St. Andrews Hall. In a strategic move supporting the Southern delegates, Caleb Cushing ruled that to be nominated by the convention, the prevailing nominee would need two-thirds of all convention delegates, not just two-thirds of those present and voting. After 57 ballots and no one receiving the required two-thirds vote, the convention recessed on May 3.

The convention reconvened on June 18 at Front Street Theater in Baltimore, Maryland. This time the fight was not over the balloting, but rather focused on the credentials of delegates. The convention attempted to seat new delegates to replace the ones who had previously walked out. This move created another walkout by the Southern delegates and Cushing stepped down as chairman in protest.

Southern delegates strategized in meetings held at St. Andrews Hall, home of the Charleston Scottish Society. This hall would later be the site of South Carolina's Secession Convention in December 1860.

David Tod was placed as convention chairman and Stephen Douglas was nominated by the party on the second ballot. Herschel V. Johnson of Georgia was selected as Douglas's running mate.

The Southern delegates gathered at the Maryland Institute elsewhere in the city and chose John C. Breckenridge, a Kentuckian and the current vice president, as their nominee. Joseph Lane, a U.S. senator from Oregon, was selected as his running mate.

As if the political landscape was not complicated enough, a fourth political party was formed. Conservative members of the Whig Party and the former Know Nothing Party formed to create the Constitutional Union Party. The new party condemned the major parties for inciting differences between the different regions of the country. The rallying cry of the new party was a patriotic support of the Union.

The Constitutional Union Party convened its convention in Baltimore in May and nominated a Whig, John Bell of Tennessee, for president and Edward Everett of Massachusetts for vice president. The slogan of the party was "The Union as it is, the Constitution as it is."

Charleston and Fort Sumter in the Civil War

John Breckinridge, the fourteenth vice president of the United States, became the nominee of the Southern Democrats for president in 1860. *Courtesy of the Library of Congress.*

The Republican National Convention was held in May in Chicago at the Wigwam convention center. New York Senator William Seward was favored to win the nomination and led through the first two ballots against twelve challengers. On the first ballot, Seward had 173½ votes of the required 233 needed for nomination. Abraham Lincoln was second, with 102 votes.

On the second ballot, votes previously cast for Senator Simon Cameron of Pennsylvania and former Congressman Edward Bates of Missouri moved to Lincoln. While only three votes now separated Seward and Lincoln, neither had the 233 votes needed. On the third ballot, many candidates stepped aside and their votes went to Lincoln, though he finished still 1½ votes shy. Delegates from Ohio announced the change of their vote, and this created a huge movement to Lincoln on the "corrected" third ballot, who was nominated by the Republicans for president. Senator Hannibal Hamlin of Maine was selected as Lincoln's running mate.

The Republican Party platform included a provision to stop the spread of slavery to the territories and the continuance of protective tariffs.

The stage was set for a Republican victory in the presidential election. With the Democrats split into two groups, North and South, and Bell siphoning away votes in the South and border states, Lincoln had a clear path to the White House.

The Union Is Dissolved!

Senator William Seward led the voting after the first two ballots at the Republican National Convention. *Courtesy of the Library of Congress.*

As predicted, the contest in the North was between Lincoln and Douglas. In the South, it was between Breckinridge and Bell. The voter turnout in the 1860 election was the second highest in the history of the United States, at 81.2 percent of registered voters, second only to the 1876 election.

Lincoln was not on the ballot in nine Southern states, and he placed last of the four candidates in five other states that permitted slavery. Breckinridge was the leading candidate in all the states that would later form the Confederacy except Virginia and Tennessee.

Lincoln did win a majority of the electoral votes, which was required to be elected president. He did not, however, receive a majority of the popular vote. The final results of the election were:

Candidate	Electoral Votes	Percentage	Popular Vote	Percentage
Abraham Lincoln	180	59%	1,865,908	39.9%
John Breckinridge	72	24%	848,019	18.1%
John Bell	39	13%	590,901	12.5%
Stephen Douglas	12	4%	1,380,201	29.5%

Charleston and Fort Sumter in the Civil War

The election of Abraham Lincoln as president incensed the Southern states. *Courtesy of the Library of Congress.*

In the presidential election, the Democratic votes were split between Stephen Douglas, candidate for the Northern Democrats, and John C. Breckinridge, candidate for the Southern Democrats.

Of all the states in the Union, only the people of South Carolina did not vote in the election. South Carolina followed a standing tradition by allowing the state legislature to determine how the electoral votes of the state would be cast, which in 1860 were for Breckinridge.

William Tecumseh Sherman, serving at a military academy in Louisiana, wrote, "Of course there were no votes for Lincoln [in Louisiana]. I would have preferred Bell but I do not think he has a chance, and I do not wish to be subject to any political conditions." Sherman chose not to vote in the election. Anticipating that the South might secede, Sherman asserted, "Secession must result in civil war, anarchy and ruin to our present form of government."

A large crowd gathered in Charleston through the night to await the results of the election. As reports were received by telegraph operators, notices were posted on a board outside the offices of the *Mercury*. Robert Barnwell Rhett Jr., the editor, held the November 7 edition until the results were certain.

Charlestonians gathered at city hall to receive the news of Lincoln's election on November 7, 1860. In protest, the state's Palmetto Flag was raised and the governor and the council of South Carolina began deliberating in secret sessions to plan for secession.

By 4:00 a.m., the results were in and the *Mercury* went to press announcing Lincoln's election. Everyone had anticipated Lincoln's election, but the confirmation of the news would set the move to secession in motion. When the news was received, "the crowd gave expression to their feelings by long and continued cheering for a Southern Confederacy. The greatest excitement prevailed, and the news spread with lightning rapidity over the city." At noon on November 7, Rhett unfurled a Palmetto Flag in front of the *Mercury*'s offices.

Across the street from city hall, Federal Judge Andrew G. Magrath had the District Court Grand Jury in session. When the day's business was concluded, Magrath addressed the court:

> *In the political history of the United States an event has happened of ominous import to the 15 slave-holding states. The State of which we are*

Charleston and Fort Sumter in the Civil War

On November 7, Federal Judge Andrew G. Magrath announced his resignation in protest of Lincoln's election. He was appointed secretary of state for the Republic of South Carolina and was the last Confederate governor of the state until Sherman marched through to burn Columbia.

citizens has always been understood to have deliberately fixed its purpose, whenever that event shall happen. Feeling an assurance of what will be the action of the state, I consider it my duty, without delay, to prepare to obey its wishes. That preparation is made by the resignation of the office I have held. For the last time I have, as a judge of the United States, administered the laws of the United States, within the limits of the State of South Carolina.

With his speech concluded, Magrath thanked the jury and officers of the court, removed his robe and left the bench. District Attorney James Connor and Port Collector W.F. Colcock also announced their resignations. Magrath stated, "We are about to sever our relations with others, because they have broken their covenant with us." Colcock was even more pointed, announcing, "I will not serve under the enemy of my country." In the minute book of the Washington Light Infantry, the secretary recorded, "The tea has been thrown overboard—the revolution of 1860 has been initiated."

After Lincoln's election was announced in Charleston on November 7, Governor Gist announced his intent to raise ten thousand volunteers and to convene a state convention to consider the question of secession.

The Union Is Dissolved!

Three days later, U.S. Senator James Chesnut followed Magrath's lead and resigned his seat in the Senate. Normally cautious and reserved, Chesnut was adamant in stating, "A line of enemies is closing around us which must be broken. For myself, I would unfurl the Palmetto flag…determined to live or die as became our ancestors. I would ring the clarion note of defiance in the insolent ears of our foe…It is your duty…to withdraw. It is your only safety."

Initially, fellow U.S. Senator James Hammond opposed secession. Hammond, in a thirty-four-page letter, suggested that Lincoln's election alone was not sufficient to merit withdrawal from the Union. Three days later, he reversed himself and resigned.

In a letter to a family member, Hammond wrote: "I thought Magrath and all those fellows were great apes for resigning and have done it myself. It is an epidemic and very foolish. It reminds me of the Japanese who when insulted rip open their own bowels…People are wild."

In an editorial in the *Mercury*, Robert Barnwell Rhett asserted:

> *There exists a great mistake…in supposing that the people of the United States are, or ever have been, one people. On the contrary, never did the sun shine on two peoples as thoroughly distinct as the people of the North and…South…Like all great nations of antiquity we are slaveholders and understand free governments. The North does not. They are a people wrapped up in selfishness. They have no idea of free government. Their idea of free government is this, that when three men get together, the two are to rule the one; when five men get together, the three are to rule the other two.*

The city was abuzz with a mix of excitement over the coming secession and anger over Lincoln's election. One Charlestonian wrote, "This past week has been one continued scene of excitement." When the new issue of *Harper's Weekly* arrived bearing an engraving of Lincoln on the cover, all of Charleston's bookstores and newsstands returned the issue.

Prior to the election, both *Harper's Weekly* and *Frank Leslie's Illustrated News* preferred Seward or Douglas to Lincoln, but after the election *Harper's* published a series of editorials strongly supporting Lincoln. Charlestonians were so infuriated over *Harper's* coverage of Lincoln's election that correspondents known to work for the New York newspaper were refused admittance to the city.

Leslie's gained favor by remaining cautious about Lincoln, and its reporters were still welcomed in the city. The newspaper chose to send an Englishman, William Waud, to cover the events in Charleston, thinking that his obvious accent might open doors for him in the city, given England's support for the South.

CHAPTER 4

A SOUTHERNER IN CHARGE

On November 9, Governor Gist, anticipating secession, issued orders to mount a guard outside the U.S. Arsenal in Charleston, "for the purpose of preventing the removal of arms and ammunition by the officers and privates in the Armory in charge thereof." One officer and twenty-two men from the Washington Light Infantry were posted to the armory, the first of any Charleston militia to report.

On November 10, following the call by the governor, the South Carolina General Assembly called for a Secession Convention.

F.J. Porter, assistant adjutant general, was sent to Charleston to assess the condition of the garrison at Fort Moultrie and the condition of the Federal fortifications throughout the harbor. On November 11, he filed his report with Colonel S. Cooper in Washington. Of the troops at Fort Moultrie, he reported:

> *The officers—Lieutenant Talbot in delicate health excepted—are in good health, and capable of enduring the fatigues incident to any duty that may be demanded of them. They are sober, intelligent, and active, and appear acquainted with their general duties, perform them with some exceptions punctually and promptly, and all are anxious to give the commanding officer the aid to which he is entitled.*
>
> *The non-commissioned officers and privates appear intelligent and obedient, but do not move with an alacrity and spirit indicating the existence of a strict discipline.*

In reporting the condition of the fort itself, Porter noted, "The unguarded state of the fort invites attack, if such design exists, and much discretion and prudence are required on the part of the commander to restore the proper security without exciting a community prompt to misconstrue actions of authority."

Porter expressed his concern over the amount of munitions held at the city arsenal but acknowledged the difficulty of getting those supplies to Fort Moultrie without exciting the populace in Charleston.

Porter also acknowledged that Fort Sumter was not yet complete and a workforce of 110 men was employed there. He did report that 39,400 pounds of powder were stored in the magazine and a total of seventy-eight guns were located in the fort.

In a private letter, financier William L. Trenholm of Charleston summarized the perplexing situation confronting the president of the United States:

> *The difficulties of Mr. Buchanan's position will be very great…If he suffers the revenue collection of this port to cease, he virtually annuls the tariff laws of the country, and cuts off the only certain source of income to the Government…In such a case all foreign goods would naturally seek this port, to escape taxation…Whether under the circumstances the President would be justified in employing the Federal Army and Navy in supporting the revenue department. Or not is a question which I cannot determine. Upon its determination rests…the probability of a collision between South Carolina and the United States.*

On November 15, Major Robert Anderson of the First Artillery received a telegram that he would "forthwith proceed to Fort Moultrie, and immediately relieve Brevet Colonel John Gardner, Lt. Colonel of First Artillery, in command thereof." The telegram was signed "by command of Lt. General Winfield Scott."

Some may have considered Anderson to be a curious choice to send to Fort Sumter in Charleston Harbor, where secession cheers were at a fever pitch. Anderson was a Southerner, born at Soldier's Retreat near Louisville, Kentucky. He was a Southern sympathizer and a former slaveholder. Scott, however, knew Anderson well and appreciated the qualities of this quiet, reserved man that made him an excellent choice to put in the "powder keg."

Anderson was the son of Richard Clough Anderson, who served with General George Washington at the Battle of Trenton in 1776, where he was wounded several times. In 1780, Richard Anderson was stationed at Fort Moultrie and captured by the British in the siege of Charles Towne. Upon capture, he was sent to prison in St. Augustine for nine months until he was part of a prisoner exchange. At the war's end, he served as an aide to Lafayette at Yorktown.

Anderson's mother was the first cousin to Chief Justice John Marshall. His brother, William Marshall Anderson, was a western explorer, Ohio attorney

Major Robert Anderson, a Southern sympathizer, was thought by some to be an unlikely officer to send to Charleston to command Fort Moultrie. *Courtesy of the Library of Congress.*

and Confederate sympathizer. William Anderson was governor of Ohio in 1865–66 and left to attempt to establish a Confederate colony in Mexico during the short reign of Emperor Maximilian.

Robert Anderson graduated from West Point in 1825 and entered the U.S. Army as a brevet second lieutenant in the Second U.S. Artillery. He later served as a colonel of Illinois Volunteers in the Black Hawk War of 1832. It is no small irony that during this service, he commanded a young captain of the Illinois Volunteers—Abraham Lincoln.

In 1833, Anderson returned to the regular army as a first lieutenant and served in the Second Seminole War. It was during this war that he met General Winfield Scott while serving on his staff as assistant adjutant general.

Among his other notable skills, Anderson was highly regarded for his talent in artillery. In 1839, he authored *Instruction for Field Artillery, Horse and Foot.* Two years earlier, he had accepted a post as instructor of artillery at West Point. He instructed many men who would later play significant roles in the Civil War, including William Tecumseh Sherman, Braxton Bragg and P.G.T. Beauregard.

Known as "Old Fuss and Feathers" and the "Grand Old Man of the Army," Winfield Scott was the first officer since George Washington to hold the rank of lieutenant general.

Charleston and Fort Sumter in the Civil War

After leaving West Point, Anderson met a young Georgia woman in New York, Eliza "Eba" Baynard Clinch. Eba's mother was the daughter of a wealthy Georgia planter and her father was General Duncan Lamont Clinch, who had served with distinguished service in the War of 1812 and the Seminole Wars in Florida. Robert Anderson and Eba Clinch were married on March 26, 1842. General Winfield Scott gave away the bride, standing in for her father.

Anderson became frustrated with his slow advance in rank. After twenty years in the army, he had advanced no higher than captain. In the Mexican War, he continued in artillery and was severely wounded at the Battle of Molino del Rey. He finally received a brevet promotion to major. It wasn't until 1857 that Anderson received a permanent promotion to major in the First U.S. Artillery.

Typically, the post at Fort Moultrie was considered to be a plum assignment. The proximity to Charleston afforded the fort's officers every opportunity to enjoy the social life and the arts to be found in the city. William Tecumseh Sherman served at Fort Moultrie from 1842 to 1846. While stationed there, the daughter of a James Island planter caught his eye and he would row across the harbor on many a Sunday afternoon to call on Miss Lawton and dine with her family. Anderson had served at Fort Moultrie for a brief time early in his career. He was familiar with the harbor and had some friends in Charleston.

In mid-November, Anderson attempted to withdraw munitions from the U.S. Arsenal in Charleston. Governor Gist quickly strengthened the guard outside the arsenal to prevent a repeat attempt. Anxious to avoid a confrontation, the presence of an armed guard kept Anderson out and essentially imprisoned the arsenal storekeeper, F.C. Humphreys, and the fourteen Federal troops stationed there.

After settling in with his new command, Anderson filed his report to Colonel Cooper, the adjutant general in Washington, on November 23.

I need not say how anxious I am—indeed, determined, so far as honor will permit—to avoid collision with the citizens of South Carolina. Nothing, however, will be better calculated to prevent bloodshed than our being found in such attitude that it would be madness and folly to attack us. There is not so much of feverish excitement as there was last week, but there is a settled determination to leave the Union, and to obtain possession of this work, is apparent to all…The clouds are threatening, and the storm may break upon us at any moment.

If we neglect, however, to strengthen ourselves, she [South Carolina] will, unless these works are surrendered on their first demand, most

Pictured in this *Harper's Weekly* engraving are Anderson and his officers. *Seated, left to right*: Captain Abner Doubleday, Major Robert Anderson, Assistant Surgeon Samuel W. Crawford and Captain John G. Foster. *Standing, left to right*: Captain Truman Seymour, First Lieutenant George W. Snyder, First Lieutenant Jefferson C. Davis, Second Lieutenant Richard K. Meade and First Lieutenant Theodore Talbot.

> *assuredly immediately attack us...I will thank the Department to give me special instructions, as my position here is rather a politico-military than a military one.*

In his next report, dated November 28, Anderson wrote of Fort Moultrie, "There appears to be a romantic desire urging South Carolinians to have possession of this work, which was so nobly defended by their ancestors in 1776; and the State, if she determines to act on the aggressive, will exert herself to take this work." He then presented Col. Cooper with the full report of his personnel at Fort Moultrie: commissioned officers, seven; band, eight; noncommissioned staff, two; noncommissioned officers, seventeen; privates, forty-eight. He concluded by noting that this force was too modest in size for a fortification like Fort Moultrie, even in peacetime. Given the current tensions in Charleston, he offered that his manpower was woefully short.

CHAPTER 5

"THE SPIRIT HAS DEPARTED"

Even prior to Lincoln's election, South Carolina Governor William H. Gist began corresponding with other Southern governors, hoping to garner support for secession. He strongly preferred that another state take the lead in secession, fearing that South Carolina's reputation for political extremism might deter other states from joining the movement.

South Carolina leaders, increasingly concerned over being perceived as hot-headed and arrogant, favored Georgia to lead the secession movement. William Henry Trescot, a South Carolinian and former assistant secretary of state for the Buchanan administration, wrote to South Carolina Congressman William Porcher Miles that Georgia must lead this movement to secure support among the Southern states: "Give her [Georgia] all the glory...We must cut up by the roots some home ambitions and much home selfishness." Meanwhile, other South Carolinians favored Alabama to take the lead, to which South Carolina Congressman Lawrence Keitt responded, "If we wait for Alabama, we will wait eternally."

Robert Barnwell Rhett and his son, editor of the Charleston *Mercury*, had long held that if any one state was bold enough to secede, the rest of the South would surely follow. By the time Lincoln was elected, South Carolinians were losing patience. Representatives from Mississippi and Alabama indicated that their respective states would follow South Carolina in secession.

U.S. Secretary of War John B. Floyd sent Assistant Adjutant General Major D.C. Buell to Charleston to meet with the civil authorities in Charleston. Buell met with Major Charles Macbeth and reported to Floyd that "all seemed determined, as far as their influence or power extends, to prevent an attack by a mob on our fort; but all are equally decided in the opinion that the forts must be theirs after secession."

THE UNION IS DISSOLVED!

Several days later, Buell met with Anderson at Fort Moultrie, informing him that Floyd was not going to send reinforcements to Charleston. He did, however, make it clear to Anderson that while he was not to do anything to provoke the authorities in Charleston, he was to "hold possession of the forts in this harbor, and if attacked you are to defend yourself to the last extremity." Buell acknowledged to Anderson that due to the small size of his force he likely could not occupy any more than one of the three forts in the harbor.

Anderson was in an untenable situation. His own government would not reinforce him. President Buchanan was a lame duck awaiting Lincoln's inauguration, and he was indecisive about his management of the situation. Anderson was responsible to the secretary of war, but since Lincoln's election, rumors abounded that Floyd, a Southerner himself, had changed his views to favoring secession. U.S. Secretary of State Lewis Cass of Michigan was furious over President Buchanan's refusal to reinforce Anderson and failure to mobilize the U.S. military to avert secession.

On December 11, the South Carolina legislature, after seven ballots, elected Francis W. Pickens as governor of South Carolina. Pickens had recently returned from Russia, where he had represented the United States. He previously served in Congress, where his thinking and principles were closely aligned with the South Carolina statesman John C. Calhoun. In short, he was an ardent supporter of states' rights. In his inaugural speech, he pledged that the state would "open her ports free to the tonnage and trade of all nations" once secession occurred.

The Northern newspapers were quick to react. The *Chicago Times*, in an editorial echoing the sentiments of most of the Northern press, wrote:

> *In one single blow our foreign commerce must be reduced to less than one-half what it now is. Our coastwise trade would pass into other hands. One-half of our shipping would lie idle at our wharves. We should lose out trade with our South, with its immense profits. Our manufactories would be in utter ruins. Let the South adopt the free-trade system, or that of a tariff for revenue, and these results would likely follow. If protection be wholly withdrawn from our labor, it could not compete, with all the prejudices against it, with the labor of Europe. We should be driven from the market, and millions of our people would be compelled to go out of employment.*

As South Carolina moved closer to secession, feelings across the country, North and South, were hardening. Louis T. Wigfall, U.S. senator from Texas, remarked on the floor of the Senate on December 12, "I would save this

Francis W. Pickens, the grandson of a South Carolina Revolutionary War hero, was an experienced politician, having served in the South Carolina legislature and Congress. He was completing a two-year term as ambassador to Russia when he was elected governor.

Union if I could; but it is my deliberate conviction that it cannot now be done…The cold sweat of death is upon it. Your Union is now dead; your Government is now dead…The spirit has departed, and it has gone back to those who gave it—the sovereign States."

Professor C.B. Haddock wrote John Crittenden, U.S. senator from Kentucky, on December 18 of the pending crisis, offering,

The steamship *John P. King* was built to run passenger service from New York to Charleston. In an act of arson, the ship was burned at the dock in New York.

The greatest danger at this moment arises from the mutual ignorance of the South and North of each other's feelings and purposes...great mistakes have been made, and great mischiefs have been done by both parties...The country is on the brink of disunion, and of disaster and misery of which no man can measure the magnitude or foretell the end.

Feelings about the coming crisis in the country were running hot, not just in the South but in the North as well. There was a brisk business of transporting both passengers and goods between Charleston and New York. In mid-December, a new 1,600-ton steamship, *John P. King*, made its maiden voyage from Charleston to New York.

As the ship docked in New York, rumors abounded that the ship would shortly fly the secession flag of South Carolina rather than the United States flag. On December 18, a fire broke out on the ship while it was tied to the docks. Unable to control the expanding blaze, the steamship was towed out to deep water to save the docks and nearby ships. The *John P. King* was a total loss. The South Carolina investors and owners asserted that the ship had fallen victim to disgruntled arsonists.

The South Carolina legislature set the date of December 6 for the election of delegates to attend a convention to consider the future course of action

Charleston and Fort Sumter in the Civil War

In December 1860, the hotels of Charleston were again filled to capacity when the Secession Convention moved to the city.

for South Carolina. The convention, made up of 169 delegates, convened in Columbia at the Baptist Church on December 17. Concerns over a smallpox outbreak forced the convention to move to Charleston the next day.

The delegates arrived in Charleston by train, where they were greeted at the station by a fifteen-gun salute. The atmosphere was festive, and many citizens turned out as the delegates were escorted by Citadel cadets to the hotels in the city.

The same day, Pickens ordered the gunboats *Nina* and *Emma* to patrol between Fort Moultrie and Fort Sumter. The boats, manned by squads from the Washington Light Infantry, were there to prevent additional Federal troops that might reinforce Anderson and to ensure that Anderson did not move his garrison to the stronger position at Fort Sumter.

The convention first met at the South Carolina Institute Hall on Meeting Street, where the Democratic convention had been held in April, but later moved to St. Andrews Hall.

David F. Jamison from Barnwell, a cotton planter, was elected president of the convention. He was not only a successful planter but also a talented writer, frequently contributing articles to *Southern Quarterly*, *Southern & Western* and *Russell's Magazine*. He also brought military credentials to the position with his service to the South Carolina Cavalry, serving as a brigadier general.

The Union Is Dissolved!

Cotton planter D.F. Jamison served as president of the Secession Convention of South Carolina. He would later serve as secretary of war for the Republic of South Carolina.

Jamison appointed John A. Inglis, Robert Barnwell Rhett, James Chesnut Jr., James L. Orr, Maxcy Gregg and W.F. Hutson to draft "an ordinance proper to be adopted by the convention." The ordinance was pointed and brief:

We the people of the State of South Carolina, in Convention assembled, do declare and ordain, and it is hereby declared and ordained, that the Ordinance adopted by us in Convention of the twenty-third day of May, in the year of our Lord one thousand seven hundred and eighty-eight, whereby the Constitution of the United States was ratified, and also all Acts and parts of Acts, of the General Assembly of this State, ratifying amendments of the said Constitution, are hereby repealed; and that the union now subsisting between South Carolina and other States, under the name of "The United States of America" is hereby dissolved.

Charleston Episcopal priest Reverend A. Toomer Porter, in his 1898 autobiography, recalls the vote on the Ordinance of Secession at 1:15 p.m. on December 20: "The ordinance of secession was read, and a stillness that could be felt prevailed…Yea after yea, was answered until every name was called, and the vote was unanimous." The delegates elected to secede from the United States and form the Republic of South Carolina for the second time in its history.

Immediately, telegraph operators began sending the expected news all through the country. The *Mercury* did not wait for the secession ordinance to be signed before it issued an "Extra." The small circular, three columns wide but the length of a normal paper, announced, "The Union Is Dissolved!" The news also quickly reached Anderson at Fort Moultrie. He immediately sent a message to Washington that the Ordinance of Secession had passed.

The bells in church towers throughout the city began to ring in celebration of the event. J.D. Pope encountered James Petigru, a well-respected Charlestonian and staunch Unionist. As they neared each other on Broad Street, the bells at St. Michael's began to peel, the usual signal for a fire. Petigru asked, "Where's the fire?" Pope responded, "Mr. Petigru, there is no fire; those are the joy bells ringing in honor of the passage of the Ordinance of Secession." Petigru responded with indignation: "I tell you there is a fire; they have this day set a blazing torch to the temple of constitutional liberty and, please God, we shall have no more peace forever."

After the passage of the Ordinance of Secession, the convention recessed until that evening, when the delegates reconvened at 6:30 p.m. at the South Carolina Institute Hall for the signing ceremony. The General Assembly and many other officials were invited to witness the historic event. Reverend Dr. John Bachman opened the evening session with a prayer. Reverend Bachman, pastor of St. John's Lutheran Church in Charleston, was a highly regarded theologian. He was a noted naturalist and friend of John James Audubon's. In fact, after many visits by the Audubon family to Charleston, their friendship blossomed into Audubon's two sons marrying Bachman's daughters.

Reverend Dr. John Bachman, pastor of St. John's Lutheran Church in Charleston, offered a prayer on the ratification of the Ordinance of Secession.

Bachman was a social reformer who ministered to African American slaves. He used his knowledge of natural history to espouse theories that blacks and whites are the same species. Despite his reformer views, Bachman also strongly favored secession and was a popular choice to offer a prayer on the passage of the Ordinance of Secession.

The *Mercury* reported of the event:

> *In the midst of deep silence, an old man, with bowed form and hair as white as snow, the Rev. Dr. Bachman, advanced forward, with upraised hands, in prayer to the Almighty God, for his blessings and favor in this great act of his people about to be consumated. The whole assembly at once rose to its feet, and, with hats off, listened to the touching and eloquent appeal to the All-Wise Dispenser of events.*

The state attorney general, Isaac W. Hayne, confirmed that he had affixed the seal of the State of South Carolina to the ordinance document. Convention President Jamison then announced that the ordinance was ready to be signed.

The ordinance was presented on a table near Jamison, and as each district in the state was called, the delegates from that district signed the document. Mrs. F.G. de Fontaine later wrote of the signing ceremony:

> *When R.B. Rhett, the "father of secession," knelt and bowed his head in silent prayer over the document he was about to sign, there was scarcely a dry eye in the house, and the excitement was so intense that fully fifteen minutes elapsed before the next signature was affixed. Two of the members who had walked arm in arm upon the platform were discussing the matter later in the evening when one remarked, "Yes, we have signed it in ink, but many of us will seal it in blood." They both became Colonels of regiments, and were killed in the same battle not ten feet apart.*

Once all the signatures were complete, President Jamison announced to the great gathering, "The Ordinance of Secession has been signed and ratified, and I proclaim the State of South Carolina an Independent Commonwealth." The signing ceremony lasted two hours, after which grand celebrations erupted across the city.

When the business of the secession convention was complete, South Carolina's six congressmen all resigned their offices. In its December 22 issue, *Harper's Weekly* offered a tribute to the six congressmen and two senators from the Palmetto State:

Above: William Waud, a correspondent for *Frank Leslie's Illustrated Newspaper*, offered this view of the celebration in Charleston when the Ordinance of Secession passed on December 20.

Right: All of South Carolina's delegation to Washington had resigned their seats by the end of the state's Secession Convention. Pictured in this *Harper's Weekly* engraving are, *from top left*: Congressmen Lawrence M. Keitt, John McQueen and Milledge L. Bonham; *from middle left*: Senators James Chesnut and James Hammond; and *from bottom left*: Congressmen William W. Boyce, John D. Ashmore and William Porcher Miles.

Personally, as well as politically, this exodus from the national halls of legislation will be felt; although for some of the Palmetto delegation have, at times, used harsh words in debate, they leave no enemies behind them. Gallant gentlemen, with high endowments, manly attributes and an integrity upon which suspicion has never even dared to glance, they carry with them kind wishes and sincere regrets, even of those who go so far to believe that "secession is treason."

CHAPTER 6

IN THE DARK
OF THE NIGHT

Now that South Carolina had formally seceded from the Union, Anderson expressed his valid concerns about his current post at Fort Moultrie.

> *We have, within 160 yards of our walls, sand hills which command our works, and which afford admirable sites for batteries, and the finest cover for sharpshooters; and that, besides this, there are numerous houses, some of them within pistol-shot, you will at once see that, if attacked in force, headed by any one but a simpleton, there is a scarce possibility of our being able to hold out.*

Fearful that any communication to the secretary of war about his intentions would be betrayed, Anderson secretly began making preparations to move his garrison. His first step was to safely secure the women and children. He informed authorities in Charleston that he intended to move the women and children to Fort Johnson on James Island. A schooner picked them up on the afternoon of December 26. In addition to the families, Anderson also smuggled supplies aboard that would be needed in Fort Sumter.

The families were escorted by Lieutenant Norman Hall as they boarded the ship. The schooner sailed to James Island but stopped short of the docks at Fort Johnson and anchored in the harbor.

At dusk, Anderson assembled his officers for a meeting, informing his men of his intention to move to Fort Sumter. Only Lieutenant Hall, escorting the women and children, and Captain John Foster, responsible for bringing several boats to move the troops, knew of Anderson's plans. Anderson announced to the group that he planned to secretly move the garrison to Fort Sumter that night. He instructed them to have their men ready and assembled in twenty minutes.

The Union Is Dissolved!

Commanding two incomplete companies of regular artillery, Anderson's garrison at Fort Moultrie on Sullivan's Island included sixty-one men, seven officers and thirteen musicians.

First Lieutenant Jeff Davis and Captain John Foster were ordered to remain at Fort Moultrie with eleven men to protect the movement of the troops. They readied five Columbiads to fire on any ship that might intercept Anderson and the garrison.

Before the Federal troops left, Anderson had them spike all the guns at Fort Moultrie except for the five made ready by Davis and Foster. Knowing that the South Carolina gunboats typically began patrolling around 9:00 p.m., he determined to move his troops shortly after 6:00 p.m. As Anderson was ready to depart Fort Moultrie, he cut down the flagstaff, declaring, "No other flag but the Stars and Stripes shall ever float from that staff."

Anderson had his men dress as if they were workers heading to Fort Sumter. All of their muskets and rifles were covered so as not to betray them as soldiers. When all the men had disembarked at their new post, two shots were fired to signal Hall to proceed to Fort Sumter with the women and children. Like the Federal soldiers, the families arrived undetected. Their schooner also carried four months' of rations and munitions.

As soon as he landed at Fort Sumter, Anderson penned his report to Adjutant General Cooper, stating,

Charleston and Fort Sumter in the Civil War

I have the honor to report that I have just completed, by the blessings of God, the removal to this fort of all of my garrison, except the Surgeon, four non-commissioned officers and seven men. We have one year's supply of hospital stores and about four month's supply of provisions for my command...I have sent orders to Captain Foster, who remains at Fort Moultrie to destroy all the ammunition which he cannot send over. The step which I have taken was, in my opinion, necessary to prevent the effusion of blood.

The remaining few men left at Fort Moultrie spiked the last guns and set fire to the fort before proceeding to Fort Sumter as well. The soldiers arriving at Fort Sumter were confronted by the workers in the fort, many of them wearing blue secession cockades. Captain Doubleday put the workers under guard until the secessionists could be sorted out and sent by boats back to the mainland.

At dawn on December 27, Charlestonians could see smoke rising at Fort Moultrie. No one had contemplated that Anderson would move his garrison. Initially, the authorities assumed that Anderson was fighting a fire and they sent two fire companies to assist him.

Word quickly returned to Charleston that the Federal troops were not present at Fort Moultrie and they had been deceived. Furious with the

As soon as the Federal troops were secure, a signal was fired to alert the nearby schooner carrying the troops' wives and children to join them at Fort Sumter.

Anderson moved his troops to Fort Sumter during the night of December 26.

While preparing to transfer his command to Fort Sumter, Anderson ordered the guns at Fort Moultrie to be spiked so that they could not be used against him by the South Carolinians.

move, Pickens denounced Anderson and asserted that the move to Fort Sumter was an "act of war."

An eyewitness in Fort Sumter on the morning of December 27 filed this report with *Harper's Weekly*:

A short time before noon, Major Anderson assembled the whole of his little force, with the workmen employed on the fort, around the foot of the flag-staff. The national ensign was attached to the cord, and Major Anderson, holding the end of the lines in his hands, knelt reverently down. The officers, soldiers, and men clustered around, many of them on their knees, all deeply impressed with the solemnity of the scene. The chaplain made an earnest prayer—such an appeal for support, encouragement, and mercy, as one would make who felt that "Man's extremity is God's opportunity." As the earnest, solemn words of the speaker ceased, the men responded Amen with a fervency that perhaps they had never before experienced, Major Anderson drew the "Star Spangled Banner" up to the top of the staff, the band broke out with the national air of "Hail Columbia" and loud and exultant cheers, repeated again and again were given by the officers, soldiers and workmen.

Anderson was a deeply religious man. At noon on December 27, he assembled his men on the parade grounds for a prayer by the chaplain, followed by the raising of the United States flag.

THE UNION IS DISSOLVED!

This engraving published in *Harper's Weekly* was drawn by an officer in Anderson's garrison. It clearly depicts the unfinished nature of the fort when Anderson took possession.

Fort Sumter, named for Revolutionary War hero General Thomas Sumter, was built as part of a long series of coastal defenses after the War of 1812. The fort was constructed on a sand bank referred to on the navigation charts as "Middle Ground." Using granite from Maine, it took ten years to create the "island" for the construction of the fort.

The walls of the fort were brick and masonry, built in three levels totaling 40 feet in height, and were 8 to 12 feet thick. The longest wall in the fort, at 350 feet, the gorge, faced to the south generally at Morris Island and James Island. The other four walls were 200 feet each and, with the gorge, formed a pentagon. Over the many years, the shipping channel to the inner harbor had shifted close to Morris, where it passed within one thousand yards of Cummings Point on the north end of Morris Island. The channel passed Fort Sumter and turned in between Fort Sumter and Fort Moultrie on Sullivan's Island. Fort Sumter was perfectly placed to restrict access to Charleston Harbor from the sea.

The first level was designed for forty-two-pound Paixhan guns, the second level for eight- to ten-inch Columbiads and the top level for mortars and twenty-four-pound guns. While Fort Sumter afforded Anderson a better position for the defense of his garrison, the fort was not oriented properly for the pending confrontation. Fort Sumter was designed to fend off an

Charleston and Fort Sumter in the Civil War

Fort Sumter was built as part of a chain of coastal defenses following the War of 1812. The masonry fort was named for South Carolina's Revolutionary War hero, General Thomas Sumter.

In addition to the numerous gun emplacements, powder magazine and barracks, Fort Sumter was constructed to provide spacious living quarters for the officers and their families.

attack from the sea and prevent an attacking fleet from entering the harbor. Anderson's aggressors, however, were already in the harbor and would be firing on him from the rear of Fort Sumter.

Anderson's report after landing at Fort Sumter would not reach Washington until December 29. On December 27, Secretary of War Floyd telegrammed Anderson: "Intelligence has reached here this morning that you have abandoned Fort Moultrie, spiked your guns, burned the carriages, and gone to Fort Sumter. It is not believed because there is no order for any such movement. Explain the meaning of this report."

Pickens sent Colonel Johnson Pettigrew and Major Ellison Capers to present his demand that Anderson immediately remove his garrison from Fort Sumter. Anderson politely refused the request.

The minute book of the Washington Light Infantry reflects the anxiety and excitement in the city over Anderson's move:

> *News of the clandestine removal of Major Anderson from Fort Moultrie to Fort Sumter, and the destruction of gun carriages, spiking of guns, etc., in Fort Moultrie caused considerable stir among the Citizens and particularly our members, who besieged the office of our worthy Captain until two o'clock, awaiting orders to take the field. At last the orders arrived for our assemblage on the Citadel Green immediately in service uniform, and in an incredibly short time some ninety rank and file were on the ground awaiting orders to march—none knew where—most believing that Fort Sumter was the point of attack. All seemed eager and fully prepared for the conflict, which was expected as a certainty.*

CHAPTER 7

BIG RED

Governor Pickens ordered the South Carolina troops to immediately take Fort Moultrie on Sullivan's Island, Fort Johnson on James Island and Castle Pinckney on Shute's Folly in the middle of the inner harbor.

The Washington Light Infantry first reached Castle Pinckney. Three companies, commanded by Colonel Johnson Pettigrew, boarded the gunboat *Nina* to reach the small island. Pettigrew found only one officer, his family and several workmen at the fortification. Anticipating the seizure, Lieutenant Richard Meade had spiked the guns in his charge. The ammunition was previously removed, likely sent to Anderson at Fort Sumter. When the flag of the *Nina* was raised over Castle Pinckney, it was the first time that a secessionist flag was raised over a United States fortification.

Once Castle Pinckney was secure, the *Nina* and the *General Clinch* transported South Carolina troops to Fort Moultrie. The Palmetto Flag flying on the *General Clinch* was transferred to fly over Fort Moultrie. When the troops arrived, only a few civilian workmen were present.

It was no small irony that a paddle-wheel steamship named the *General Clinch* took the secessionists to Fort Moultrie. Major Anderson was married to the daughter of General Clinch, a Georgia planter, politician and officer.

Robert W. Barnwell, James H. Adams and James L. Orr were sent by Pickens to Washington to meet with President Buchanan. Their letter to Buchanan, dated December 28, notified the president that South Carolina considered the forts, magazines, lighthouses and other Federal real estate to be the property of the state. They urged Buchanan to immediately withdraw the Federal troops from Charleston.

Buchanan responded with a lengthy letter indicating that he could not and would not withdraw his troops. He ended his response by affirming that "it is my duty to defend Fort Sumter...against hostile attacks...I do

This page: Charleston was home to as many as fifty militia units, some of them serving as volunteer fire companies prior to South Carolina's secession. Pictured in these engravings are the Washington Light Infantry and the Charleston Zouaves.

Colonel J.J. Pettigrew boarded the guard boat *Nina* with three companies and captured Castle Pinckney first. The flag of the *Nina*, a red flag bearing a single white star, became the first secession flag to be raised over a United States fort.

Castle Pinckney, located on Shute's Folly in the middle of the harbor, was armed with twenty-eight large guns, which were later transferred to the many Confederate batteries that would surround Anderson and his garrison at Fort Sumter.

not perceive how such a defense can be construed into a menace against the city of Charleston."

On December 30, Pickens ordered the seizure of the U.S. Arsenal. Troops led by Colonel John Cunningham arrived at the site and demanded that the ordnance storekeeper, F.C. Humphreys, and the

After seizing Fort Moultrie, state troops moved usable guns to replace those spiked by Anderson's men. The fort was 1.8 miles from Fort Sumter, well within range to attack the Federal garrison. Anderson moved from Fort Moultrie because it was vulnerable to ground attack, but the fort was perfectly situated and constructed to attack Sumter or fend off attack from the sea.

Governor Pickens, accompanied by his wife and daughter, inspects the South Carolina Volunteer Troops now assembled at Fort Moultrie.

fourteen Federal troops surrender the arsenal. Humphreys issued a written response to Cunningham:

> *I am constrained to comply with your demand for the surrender of this arsenal, from the fact that I have no force for its defense. I do so, however, solemnly protesting against the illegality of this measure. I also demand, as a right, that I be allowed to salute my flag before lowering it, with one gun for each State now in the Union* [thirty-two] *and that my command be allowed to occupy these quarters assigned to them until instructions can be obtained from the War Department.*

Cunningham allowed the Federal troops the privilege of firing a salute as they lowered their flag. The seizure of the munitions at the arsenal provided plentiful muskets, rifles and munitions, enough to supply three divisions.

In late December, President Buchanan decided to take a more assertive position with his garrison at Fort Sumter and gave General Scott the orders to reinforce Anderson. Scott made preparations to send the USS *Brooklyn*,

As the Republic of South Carolina prepared for conflict, many militia units volunteered for state service and drilled on the parade grounds at The Citadel. After state troops seized the Federal arsenal on December 30, Governor Pickens had enough muskets, rifles and munitions to outfit three divisions.

commanded by Captain Farragut, to move three hundred veteran soldiers from Fort Monroe, Virginia, to Fort Sumter.

The *Brooklyn*, commissioned in 1859, was an imposing man-of-war armed with one ten-inch gun and twenty nine-inch guns. It was built to deliver damaging broadsides to an enemy and withstand attacks.

Scott later rethought his plan and decided that sending a warship was too visible and aggressive. He wanted to reinforce Fort Sumter, not be the impetus for the beginning of a war. Additionally, the *Brooklyn* had a substantial draft and the shipping channel to Charleston was known for its treacherous, shallow depth.

He finally decided that a civilian ship might be able to slip in without a lot of notice and accomplish the mission. The government chartered the *Star of the West*, a merchant steamer that typically ran routes to and from New York and New Orleans. The side-wheel steamer was known for its speed, and Scott considered that might be helpful in avoiding the newly constructed Confederate batteries in Charleston. One of his critical mistakes, though, was that he did not pause to evaluate the ability of the ship to take on fire if it was hit.

On December 31, authorities received a telegram from Secretary of the Interior Thomas of Mississippi and Senator Wigfall in Washington that Buchanan and Scott were planning to reinforce and resupply Fort Sumter. As was typically the case, there were so many secessionists still in Washington that it was most difficult for the Federal government to act without its plans being betrayed to the South.

Pickens ordered Major Peter F. Stevens, the superintendent of The Citadel, to erect a battery on Morris Island able to control the ships entering the shipping channel to Charleston Harbor. Stevens recalled students who were on leave for the Christmas holiday. Lieutenant Armstrong, on The Citadel faculty, picked the best site and, beginning on January 1, started construction on the sand battery.

Fifty student cadets were deployed to Morris Island. When the cadets arrived, they were presented with a red palmetto flag that was made for them by the women of the Vincent family, the family that owned most of Morris Island at the time. The handsome flag was described in the *Charleston Daily Courier* as a flag with a "white palmetto tree on a blood red field." This flag has since become infamous in Citadel lore, known affectionately as "Big Red."

The cadets transported twenty-four-pound siege guns from the school for use at the battery. The guns were placed behind the sand bunkers to avoid detection by passing ships. It took several days to complete the

President James Buchanan ordered the *Star of the West* to depart New York loaded with supplies and troops to resupply and reinforce Anderson at Fort Sumter. After taking on effective fire in the Charleston Harbor channel, the steamer turned back without accomplishing its mission.

preparations for the battery. While on the island, the cadets were housed in a pest house for smallpox patients on the island. The new sand battery was aptly named Fort Morris.

On January 2, Senator Wigfall sent a telegram to former Congressman Bonham in Charleston. Wigfall's message was short, but its content loomed large to South Carolina. The message read, "Holt succeeds Floyd. It means war. Cut off supplies from Anderson and take Sumter soon as possible."

The *Star of the West*, commanded by Captain John McGowan, finally left New York on January 5 loaded with arms, munitions provisions and two hundred new recruits. Assistant Adjutant General Thomas wrote to Anderson from New York on January 5. Thomas reported:

> *Sir: In accordance with the instructions of the General-in-Chief, I yesterday chartered the steamship* Star of the West *to re-enforce your small garrison with two hundred well-instructed recruits from Fort Columbus...Besides arms for the men, one hundred spare arms and all the cartridges in the arsenal on Governor's Island will be sent; likewise, three months' subsistence for the detachment and six months' desiccated and fresh vegetables, with*

three or four days' fresh beef for your entire force. Further re-enforcements
will be sent if necessary…

   Should a fire, likely to prove injurious, be opened upon any vessel bringing
re-enforcements or supplies, or upon tow boats with reach of your guns, they
may be employed to silence such fire…

   You are warned to be upon your guard against all telegrams, as false ones
may be attempted to be passed upon you.

The same day, Scott finally realized that news of the mission already
had been passed to the South Carolina authorities in Charleston. He tried
to stop the mission, but the ship had already departed. He ordered the
USS *Brooklyn* to intercept the *Star of the West*, and while Farragut made
every attempt to do so, the civilian steamer was simply too fast. The *Star of
the West* made such good time that McGowan even paused off the coast of
North Carolina to fish, and, still, the *Brooklyn* could not catch the lighter,
faster ship.

Even as the operation was planned and initiated, Anderson had never
been informed of Buchanan's orders or Scott's plans. When news did finally
reach Fort Sumter that they would be reinforced, Anderson assumed that
it was just one of the many false reports that made it to them. A workman
brought a Northern newspaper to Fort Sumter containing a story about
the *Star of the West*. The officers concluded that the story was false. It made
no sense to them that such an operation would make it to the press and
that Washington would send a civilian ship rather than a man-of-war.

Not knowing that the *Star of the West* was en route to Fort Sumter,
Anderson filed his weekly report to Adjutant General Cooper. Pickens
allowed Anderson to send his report to Washington by Anderson's brother,
Larz. He noted:

   The South Carolinians are also very active in erecting batteries and
   preparing for a conflict, which I pray God may not occur. Batteries have
   been constructed bearing upon and, I presume, commanding the entrance
   to the harbor…I shall not ask for any increase of my command, because
   I do not know what the ulterior views of the Government are. We are
   now, or soon will be, cut off from all communication, unless by means of
   a powerful fleet, which shall have the ability to carry the batteries at the
   mouth of the harbor.

The *Star of the West* arrived at the mouth of the harbor channel at
midnight on January 8. McGowan was a veteran of the U.S. Revenue

Marine, a predecessor of the Coast Guard, and was certainly skilled enough for this important mission. However, in the dark of night, with the lighthouse and harbor lights extinguished, he was not anxious to traverse the tricky shipping channel into Charleston. McGowan doused his own lights to wait for first light.

Just before daybreak, McGowan made preparations to move his ship. He was hoping that the ship would be mistaken for a coastal trade ship and not discovered until he was able to reach Fort Sumter. At 6:20 a.m., in a strong wind and cold rain, McGowan ran up his colors and the *Star of the West* began its high-speed run to reach Fort Sumter. Aware of the Confederate position at Fort Moultrie, McGowan kept his ship closer to Morris Island.

At the far north end of Morris Island at Cummings Point, McGowan's crew could see several buildings and the red palmetto flag fluttering in the wind, but could not detect the batteries at Fort Morris.

The guard boat *General Clinch* spotted the steamer entering the channel and fired signal rockets, but McGowan did not respond. The captain of the *General Clinch* then fired flares to alert the batteries of the fast-moving ship.

Cadet William S. Simkins spotted the U.S. flag displayed on the steamship and alerted the cadets and officers at Fort Morris. Major Stevens gave the order to Cadet Captain John M. Whilden to fire on the *Star of the West*. Cadet George E. "Tuck" Haynesworth pulled the lanyard on the siege gun and fired a warning shot across the bow of the ship.

Captain Doubleday was on the parapet with his spyglass that morning and watched the civilian ship flying a U.S. flag enter the harbor. He was surprised to see the Morris Island battery fire on the ship. Doubleday raced to Anderson's quarters to wake his commanding officer. Anderson ordered the drum roll to awaken his troops. None of the guns positioned to Morris Island was big enough to reach the cadets at Fort Morris.

The ship gave no signs of relenting. Cadet Samuel Pickens fired a shot that did strike the ship but did little damage. This was followed by a shot by Cadet Thomas Ferguson, which also hit the ship. The cadets fired a total of seventeen shots, with three hitting the ship. Shells hit the bow, the rudder and the ship's rigging. Anderson debated whether to enter the fight but was concerned that his actions might further exacerbate the situation. Taking on effective fire and realizing that the batteries at Fort Moultrie would quickly be in range, McGowan turned his ship to leave the harbor without reinforcing Anderson. The men aboard the *Star of the West* left confused and enraged, not understanding why Fort Sumter had not fired to support them.

Forty Citadel cadets, commanded by Major Peter Stevens, assembled at a new battery, Fort Morris, armed with four twenty-four-pound field howitzers. From this position, they could effectively fire on any ship entering the mouth of Charleston Harbor. In this *Harper's Weekly* engraving, the cadets are firing on the *Star of the West*, hitting the steamer on the bow and rudder.

Anderson was incensed over the firing on the *Star of the West*. He immediately sent Lieutenant Norman Hall, under a flag of truce, with a letter to deliver to Pickens. Hall traveled by boat in full dress uniform to present the communication. Anderson's letter read:

> *Sir: Two of your batteries fired this morning upon an unarmed vessel bearing the flag of my Government. As I have not been notified that war has been declared by South Carolina against the government of the United States, I cannot but think this hostile act was committed without your sanction or authority. Under that hope, and that alone, did I refrain from opening fire upon your batteries. I have the honor, therefore, to respectfully ask whether the above mentioned act—one, I believe, without parallel in the history of our country or any other civilized Government—was committed in obedience to your instructions, and to notify you, if it is not disclaimed, that I must regard it as an act of war; and that I shall not, after a reasonable time for the return of my passenger, permit any vessel to pass within the range of the guns of my fort. In order to save, as far as in*

After the firing on the *Star of the West*, Anderson sent a letter under a flag of truce to Governor Pickens. Pickens responded, "The act is perfectly justified by me."

my power, the shedding of blood, I beg that you will give due notification of this, my decision, to all concerned. Hoping, however, that your answer will be such as will justify a further continuance of forbearance on my part, I have the honor to be very respectfully,

Your obedient servant,
Robert Anderson
Major, First Artillery U.S.A. Commanding Fort Sumter
January 9, 1861

Pickens immediately responded with his own lengthy letter, ending it with the statement, "The act is perfectly justified by me."

CHAPTER 8

HORSES AND SPIES

The incident in Charleston Harbor had a predictable impact on both the North and the South. The North was incensed that South Carolinians had actually fired on the flag of the United States. Southerners were furious that Buchanan had attempted to reinforce Fort Sumter with additional troops and provisions. In the next three days, Mississippi, Florida and Alabama followed South Carolina in secession.

On January 10, the *Mercury* prominently ran an article about the events in the harbor.

> *Yesterday, the ninth of January, will be remembered in history. Powder has been burnt over the decree of our State, timber has been crashed, perhaps blood spilled. The expulsion of the "Star of the West" from Charleston Harbor yesterday morning was the opening of the ball of Revolution. We are proud that our harbor has been so honored. We are proud that the State of South Carolina, so long, so bitterly, and so contemptuously reviled and scoffed at, above all others, should thus proudly have thrown back the scoff of her enemies. Entrenched upon her soil, she has spoken from the mouth of her cannon, and not from the mouths of scurrilous demagogues, fanatics, and scribblers…South Carolina will stand under her own Palmetto tree, unterrified by the snarling growls or assaults of the one, undeceived or deterred by the wily machinations of the other. And if that red seal of blood be still lacking for the parchment of our liberties, and blood they want— blood they shall have—and blood enough to stamp it all in red. For, by the God of our Fathers, the soil of South Carolina shall be free!*

As it became increasingly apparent that Anderson would not agree to withdraw his troops from Charleston, Pickens stepped up his preparations

THE UNION IS DISSOLVED!

This engraving from *Harper's Weekly* depicts the steamship *Marion*, which Pickens ordered to be converted to a man-of-war to patrol Charleston Harbor.

to defend the city. On January 10, he ordered the seizure of the *Marion*, an eight-hundred-ton steamship that provided cargo and passenger service between New York and Charleston. The *Marion* was converted to a man-of-war and patrolled the harbor and shipping channel. Its principal task was to fend off any future attempts to reinforce or resupply Fort Sumter.

When the *Star of the West* returned to New York on January 12, Lieutenant Charles R. Woods, commanding the Ninth Infantry aboard ship, filed his report with the assistant adjutant general in Washington. He wrote,

> *Before we were fired upon we had discovered a red palmetto flag flying, but could see nothing to indicate there was a battery there…Finding it impossible to take my command to Fort Sumter, I was obliged most reluctantly to turn about, and try to make my way out of the harbor before my retreat should be cut off by vessels then in sight…From the preparations that had been made for us I have every reason to believe the Charlestonians were perfectly aware of our coming*

One officer aboard the *Star of the West* had a humorous take on his failed attempt to reach Fort Sumter, writing, "The people of Charleston pride themselves upon their hospitality, but it exceeded my expectations. They gave us several 'balls' before we landed."

Charleston and Fort Sumter in the Civil War

Pickens wrote a letter to President Buchanan on January 12 and presented the letter to South Carolina Attorney General I.W. Hayne. Hayne's charge was to demand the surrender of Fort Sumter. Pickens expressed his desire to avoid bloodshed if possible but was clear in stating that if Anderson stayed in Fort Sumter the only potential outcome was an attack to forcibly remove him.

Hayne stated, "I do not come as a military man to demand the surrender of a fortress, but as the legal officer of the State—its attorney general—to claim for the State the exercise of its undoubted right of eminent domain." Buchanan, of course, did not acquiesce to Pickens's and Hayne's requests.

Surprisingly, Pickens decided to allow the resumption of mail service to and from Fort Sumter. By mid-January, Charleston authorities agreed to take orders from Fort Sumter for provisions and deliver them to the fort. On January 19, the quartermaster general for the South Carolina Militia shipped two hundred pounds of beef and fresh vegetables to the fort.

On January 19, U.S. Secretary of War Holt sent a letter to David Jamison in Charleston thanking him for allowing provisions to Fort Sumter. Holt admitted to his confusion and surprise with Jamison's offer, given that neither the U.S. government nor Major Anderson had requested the supplies.

In exchange for the provisions, Jamison requested an assurance from President Buchanan that "the public peace will not be disturbed by any act of hostility toward South Carolina." Without delivering any such assurance from Buchanan, Holt simply reminded Jamison that only Congress has the power to declare war.

Hayne, still in Washington, had previously notified Federal authorities that "Major Anderson and his command do now obtain all necessary supplies, including fresh meat and vegetables, and, I believe, fuel and water, from the city of Charleston, and do now enjoy communication by post and special messenger with the President, and will continue to do so, certainly until the door to negotiation has been closed."

Holt asserted to Jamison that the Federal government was encouraged by the current cooperation. He reminded Jamison that "Major Anderson is not menacing Charleston, and I am convinced that the happiest result which can be attained is that both he and the authorities of South Carolina shall remain on their present amicable footing, neither party being bound by any obligation whatever, except the high Christian and moral duty to keep the peace, and to avoid all causes of mutual irritation."

On January 21, Anderson submitted his report to Holt that Charleston authorities were, once again, allowing confidential correspondence to travel to and from Sumter. Anderson notified Washington that work on the fort had progressed well and he now had fifty-one guns in position if needed. He detailed the work of the South Carolina Militia on Morris Island, Fort Johnson and Sullivan's Island, as observed from the walls of Fort Sumter. He wisely expressed his concern over the many sand batteries on Morris Island, understanding that shot and shell are of limited value to dislodging the Carolinians from those positions.

Though the situation in Charleston was settling into a calm routine, passions were still aflame in Congress. The debate in Washington and throughout the Southern states had now shifted from a focus on slavery as a reason for secession to a debate over the constitutional right to secession. Several key Southern states had not yet chosen secession, giving Congress even more reason to tread lightly over the debate.

On January 23, Congressman Samuel Blair of Pennsylvania offered in a speech on the House floor, "Will the generations that are to succeed us believe that at such time we sat out a whole winter with these guns still pointed at us, trying how far we might go to comply with the demands of traitors?" Senator James Grimes of Iowa took a different but equally passionate tact in a speech on the Senate floor, suggesting, "The question before the country… has become something more than an issue on the slavery question growing out of the construction of the Constitution. The issue now before us is, whether we have a country, whether or not this is a nation…Who does not see that by adopting these compromise positions we tacitly recognize the right of these States to secede?"

Congressman Samuel Cox of Ohio admonished his fellow members: "State after state secedes and yet…we still stand, like mere spectators on the shore, in helpless bewilderment." Former presidential candidate Stephen Douglas insisted that secession was "unlawful, unconstitutional, criminal," but continued to say, "South Carolina has no right to secede; but she has done it…Are we prepared for war?…I confess I am not… War is disunion, certain, inevitable, irrevocable. I am for peace to save the Union."

Congressman Thomas Corwin of Ohio was a moderate in the House and typically a peacemaker in his role as chairman of the Committee of 33, a group appointed to negotiate a resolution between the North and South. After a month of endless debate and no resolution in sight, he became disenchanted with the prospects for peace, saying,

I cannot comprehend the madness of the times. Southern men are theoretically crazy. Extreme northern men are practical fools, the latter are really quite as bad as the former. Treason is in the air around us everywhere and goes by

Charleston and Fort Sumter in the Civil War

in the name of Patriotism. Men in Congress boldly avow it, and the public offices are full of acknowledged secessionists. God alone I fear can help us.

On January 31, South Carolina Attorney General Hayne, who was still in Washington, delivered to President Buchanan another demand from Pickens to surrender Fort Sumter to the state. Hayne also delivered his own letter to the president extending an offer from the State of South Carolina to purchase Fort Sumter. Buchanan rebuffed both letters.

On January 28, South Carolina formally adopted the flag that had already been flown proudly—the Palmetto Flag, with a blue field and the white crescent in the corner. This flag had its origin, in part, as far back as banners used by protestors in South Carolina over the Stamp Act in 1765. The flag, as adopted in 1861, was first used by South Carolina troops in 1775 and is part of the lore of the Battle of Fort Sullivan on June 28, 1776. A red version of this flag was flown by Citadel cadets at Fort Morris.

The Charleston palmetto, the venerable symbol of the old, historic city.

The Union Is Dissolved!

Through January, tensions continued to mount, causing Anderson to reconsider the wisdom of having women and children in Fort Sumter. Additionally, their presence was helping to deplete the modest supply of provisions available to the garrison.

Anderson requested and received permission from Pickens on January 21 to evacuate the families to New York. On February 3, the *Marion* docked at Fort Sumter, picking up the precious cargo of the wives and children from the garrison. One of the wives would write:

> *When the ship was passing, [the fort] fired a gun and gave three heart-thrilling cheers as a parting farewell to the dear loved ones on board, whom they may possibly never meet again this side of the grave. The response was weeping and waving adieux to husbands and fathers. A small band put up in an isolated fort, completely surrounded by instruments of death, as five forts could be seen from the steamer's deck, with their guns pointing toward Sumter.*

Tensions between Governor Pickens and the Federal government continued to escalate in January. Fearing an attack, Anderson requested that Pickens allow him to evacuate the women and children from Fort Sumter. On February 3, the families were transported on the steamship *Marion* to New York.

Charleston and Fort Sumter in the Civil War

During the whirlwind of events since November, Charlestonians had not singularly focused on the possibility of war. Even though the St. Cecilia Society canceled its winter ball, the South Carolina Jockey Club announced that race week, the first week in February, would take place as usual.

Just as in prior years for a century before, race week was an intoxicating mix of sport and society. Everyone in Charleston, from slave to master, attended the races. Schools closed, courts recessed and businesses shut down for the week. Unlike in many other cities, the races in Charleston maintained an aura of social acceptability. From Wednesday to Saturday, horse races were held in the day and great dinners and balls were held at night. The "sport of kings" was the fancy of men and women alike.

Even with the tensions afoot in 1861, the Jockey Club held to its usual rule: "Respectable strangers from abroad, or from other states, are never allowed to pay admission to any stands on the course. On their arrival, they are immediately considered guests and provided with tickets."

The Jockey Club Ball, always on Friday, was the biggest event of the year for high society. Even with war looming, the great ball was no different in 1861. The menu for the dinner alone speaks for the elaborate nature of the ball: "After the soup course, four varieties of fish, nine different kinds of broiled meat or seafood, ten kinds of roasted meat, fourteen varieties of game, six vegetables, nine choices of dessert, plus four 'ornaments'" were served. The editor of the national racing magazine *The Spirit of the Times* wrote of the meal, "It would seem the entire animal and vegetable kingdom had been placed at the command of the Club's caterer and that heaven itself had furnished the cooks."

The featured match race in 1861 held a particular fascination for South Carolinians. The match race, a four-mile heat, was to feature a great Virginia stallion, Planet, the equivalent of the standing national champion that had never lost a race at that distance, versus Albine, a filly from South Carolina. Though Major T.W. Doswell, of Virginia, the owner of Planet, was well known to South Carolina horsemen, the South Carolinians were looking forward to goading the Virginians to join the secession movement. Additionally, Albine's owner, Major James DuGue Ferguson, had once sent the filly to Virginia to be trained by Doswell, but he returned her, insisting that she could never be a racehorse.

Albine was then trained by the great horse trainer Hercules, a slave at Eutaw Plantation in Upper St. John's Parish. On the day of the 1861 match race, Hercules gave careful instructions to the slave jockey to run a waiting race. Planet started off on a fast pace and Albine followed one length behind. After three miles, Albine pulled even, and with only a quarter mile to go, she pulled away, winning by several lengths. Her winning time at 7 minutes, 36½ seconds, was not only the fastest four-mile time for Charleston in a century, but it is also the standing record for four miles in the United States.

Governor Pickens attended all the festivities of the week, including the daily races. On Wednesday, opening day, he ordered all the batteries on the harbor to ready for a forty-eight-hour bombardment. On Saturday, after the great match race, he declared martial law on Sullivan's Island, causing concern with everyone that hostilities were about to commence.

After Lincoln's election in November, a Northerner, Charles D. Brigham, came to Charleston. He was working under cover for the *New York Tribune*, sending coded messages back to New York of the events in Charleston. In February, Brigham was arrested under suspicion of spying. After an appearance before Pickens, he was interrogated by Judge Magrath, who, despite his skills as an interrogator, could not get the Northerner to crack.

Brigham was then turned over to Alexander H. Brown, a well-respected criminal lawyer. Like Magrath, he could not get Brigham to talk. During the interrogation, he offered, "Mr. Brigham, while I think you are all right, this is a peculiar emergency, and you must see that, under the circumstances, it will be necessary for you to leave the south at once." Brigham was protesting the treatment when Brown asked, "Do you know who is writing the letters from here to the *Tribune*?" Brigham insisted that he did not.

Even though Brigham was gone, the reports continued to appear in the *Tribune*. What even Brigham did not know was that there were two other *Tribune* reporters undercover in Charleston at the same time. Brigham did complain that Anderson and his men, "every day and every hour in the day, been compelled to see transported within pistol shot of its battlements the huge engines that were to be used against them the moment South Carolina could say she was ready…These things have been well known to the Federal Government, and yet it had done nothing."

CHAPTER 9

THE CONFEDERATE STATES

Also in early February, Mississippi, Florida, Alabama, Georgia, Louisiana and Texas joined South Carolina in seceding from the Union. Delegates from these Southern states assembled for a convention in Montgomery, Alabama. On February 8, the convention formed the Confederate States of America.

Robert Barnwell Rhett Sr. of Charleston attended the convention, representing South Carolina with aspirations that he would be elected president of the Confederate states. However, the delegates from other states viewed Rhett to be too radical and inflexible in his views. Former U.S. Senator Jefferson Davis of Mississippi was elected as president and former U.S. Congressman Alexander Stephens of Georgia was elected vice president.

Davis was careful in structuring his cabinet, giving no state more than one position. Though Davis favored South Carolinian Robert W. Barnwell as secretary of state, the South Carolina delegation lobbied successfully for Christopher Memminger to be selected as secretary of the treasury. Davis then picked Robert Toombs of Georgia as secretary of state.

Rhett, bruised over his rejection for any significant post, was appeased by his selection to chair the committee to draft the new constitution for the new Confederate government. Within seventeen days, Rhett and his committee had completed their work and presented the constitution for approval.

The Confederate States Constitution was written in a similar form as the United States Constitution, but it also contained explicit protections of the institution of slavery while banning international slave trading. Predictably, the constitution also reserved greater powers for the states that made up the Confederate States of America, including a provision that prohibited the government from using revenues collected in one state to fund improvements in a different state.

THE UNION IS DISSOLVED!

Former U.S. Senator Jefferson Davis was selected by the Southern convention to serve as president of the Confederate States of America. *Courtesy of the Library of Congress.*

Alexander Stephens of Georgia was elected vice president of the Confederate States of America. *Courtesy of the Library of Congress.*

Jefferson Davis of Mississippi was sworn in as president of the Confederate States of America on February 18, 1861, on the steps of the capitol of Alabama.

Many delegates at the Southern convention felt that once they formed a separate government, the South would be able to negotiate a peace with the North. They believed that the businessmen in the North would never risk a disruptive war given their need for cotton. There was also a strong belief that European countries would come to the aid of the South due to the same economic needs for raw products, especially cotton.

If the result of secession was war, the delegates were prepared to wage what they viewed to be the Second War for Independence. Though they accepted that the South would face a superior number of men and arms, they were convinced that will and the ability of the Southern soldiers would overcome those obstacles.

Virginia had not yet seceded and, thus, did not attend the convention. Former President John Tyler remarked, "Virginia looks on for the present with her arms folded, but she only bides her time."

In one of his first communications as president, Davis informed Pickens that any decisions regarding Fort Sumter were now the responsibility of the

Confederate government. Even though Pickens voiced his disagreement that the authority to attack Anderson was his alone, he was glad to have the Confederate government accept control. He had previously confided to William Porcher Miles, representing South Carolina, in Montgomery, "There is danger ahead unless you give us immediately a strong organized government to take jurisdiction of all military defense."

Many secessionists, however, were concerned that Pickens would act impulsively and prematurely. While many other Southern governors admired the action taken by South Carolina, they were also concerned that if South Carolina acted against Fort Sumter before the Southern states could coalesce, the future of a Southern nation might be compromised.

While the Deep South states were meeting at the Confederate States Convention in Montgomery, Virginia was in the midst of a peace convention to determine its course of action. Former President John Tyler, a Virginian and an avowed states' rights supporter, sent a telegram to Pickens from the Virginia convention: "Can my voice reach you? If so, do not attack Fort Sumter. You know my sincerity. The Virginia delegation here earnestly unite."

CHAPTER 10

THE STUDENT ARRIVES

W hile Pickens acted and spoke more boldly, Anderson was much more cautious. He knew that the smallest mistake could be construed as an act of aggression. On February 13, he wrote Pickens to express his concern about the gunboat patrols around Fort Sumter. On the previous night, the *General Clinch* had moved too close on patrol, causing a sentinel's concern. The gunboat did not move away until the sentinel fired a warning shot with his musket. Anderson noted that "the gun-battery guard, I am happy to say, did not deem it necessary to fire." He concluded by offering, "Assuring you that every exertion will be made by me to guard against any wrong act on the part of my command, and hoping that these boats will henceforth be more particular in obeying your instructions."

Negotiations with Washington were difficult, with the sitting president about to leave office and the president-elect not to be inaugurated until March. Buchanan was not anxious to cause a war by his actions or inaction. He believed that he could not simply withdraw the Federal garrison. He once stated, "If I withdraw Anderson from Sumter I can travel home to Wheatland by the light of my own burning effigies." (Wheatland was Buchanan's estate in Lancaster County, Pennsylvania.)

Lincoln was not yet in office, and while he was greatly troubled by the developments in the South, he was not yet in a position to act. In February, an editorial in the Philadelphia *Pennsylvanian* did not exude confidence in Lincoln, stating, "The President of the Southern Confederation is a gentleman, a scholar, a soldier, and a statesman…The President Elect of the United States is neither a scholar, a soldier, nor a statesman…Without the polished elegance of the well bred man he has all the rough manners and course [*sic*] sayings of a clown."

On February 15, the Provisional Confederate Congress in Montgomery upped the ante in negotiations by voting to take Fort Sumter and Fort Pickens in Florida by force if necessary. Tyler again telegrammed Pickens on February

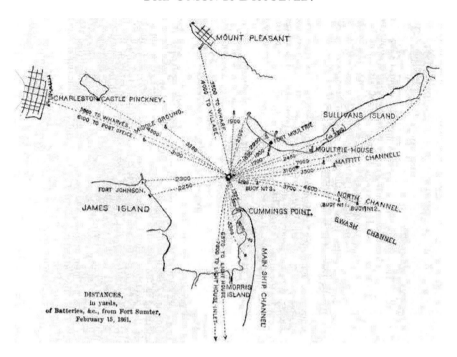

This map, drawn by a Federal officer at Fort Sumter, marked the distances of the various Confederate batteries and landmarks around Fort Sumter. *Courtesy of the Library of Congress.*

18, stating that he had a source who assured him that a former South Carolina congressman indicated that Fort Sumter would be taken by March 4. Tyler offered, "This startles the President. Will you quiet him by your reply?"

There was as much disinformation as correct intelligence during the months of negotiation. On February 20, Senator Wigfall sent an urgent telegram to Pickens, warning, "Attempt to re-enforce Anderson by stealth at night in small boats determined on."

On specific instructions of the Montgomery convention, Confederate Secretary of War Leroy P. Walker telegrammed Pickens on March 1: "This government assumes the control of the military operations at Charleston and will make demand of the fort when fully advised. An officer goes tonight to take charge." Pickens bristled at this communication, but on the advice of more moderate South Carolinians, he conceded the authority to the Confederate government.

The unnamed officer in Walker's telegram was newly appointed Brigadier General P.G.T. Beauregard. He was a dashing officer, highly regarded for his abilities as a military artillerist and tactician. Standing at five feet, six inches tall and 150 pounds, he was often referred to as "Little Napoleon."

Charleston and Fort Sumter in the Civil War

Pierre Gustave Toutant Beauregard was the first appointment as a brigadier general made by Jefferson Davis. He assumed command of all Confederate forces in Charleston on March 3, 1861.

Beauregard was born to white Creole parents at Cantreras, a sugar cane plantation in St. Bernard Parish, about twenty miles from New Orleans. He was sent by his father, Jacques Toutant-Beauregard, to schools in New Orleans and, later, to a French school in New York. It was in New York, at the age of twelve, that he learned to speak English.

Beauregard enrolled at West Point for training as a civil engineer. There he dropped the hyphen from his name and used "Toutant" as a second middle name. He preferred to be called G.T. Beauregard. He was popular with the other students, earning affectionate nicknames such as "Little Creole," "Bory," "Little Frenchman," "Felix" and "Little Napoleon."

The ambitious Creole had a natural talent for the artillery. His professor of artillery, Robert Anderson, was his favorite instructor, and the two would often dine together in the evening.

Beauregard graduated second in his class in 1838 with an outstanding record as an artilleryman and a military engineer. For a short time, he stayed on at West Point as Anderson's assistant instructor of artillery.

Leaving West Point, he accepted a commission in the U.S. Army as a second lieutenant. During the Mexican War, Beauregard served as a military engineer and was promoted to captain after the Battles of Contreras and Churubusco and to major after the Battle of Chapultepec.

Beauregard became known for his daring reconnaissance missions and his excellent strategic plans. He never hesitated to speak up when he disagreed with superiors or other officers about the proper tactics. He often swayed the general officers as he explained his own ideas for attack. He also was not shy about promoting his own talent. After the Mexican War, Beauregard wrote a book, *Personal Reminiscences of an Engineer Officer During the Campaign in Mexico under General Winfield Scott in 1847–48.*

In 1848, Beauregard accepted an appointment as chief engineer for Mississippi and Lake Defenses in Louisiana. He spent considerable time and talent repairing old fortifications and building new ones on the Florida Gulf Coast. He also improved and repaired Fort St. Philip and Fort Jackson on the Mississippi River below New Orleans.

While working as chief engineer, Beauregard patented an invention called the "self-acting bar excavator." This contraption was used by Beauregard to aid ships crossing over sandbars and clay bars in the Mississippi River.

In 1852, Beauregard supported Franklin Pierce for president of the United States. Once elected as the fourteenth president, Pierce rewarded Beauregard by appointing him as chief engineer for the New Orleans Customs House. This large granite building, built in 1848, was sinking in the unpredictable soil in New Orleans.

By 1856, Beauregard became bored with life in the military during peacetime and contemplated leaving the service. William Walker, who had been elected president of Nicaragua in a farcical election, offered Beauregard the rank of second in command of the Nicaraguan army. Walker had the financial backing of Pierre Soule', an influential New Orleans politician. It was Soule' who promoted Beauregard to Walker. Fortunately, General Winfield Scott and other officers convinced Beauregard that going to Nicaragua was folly and that he should remain in the U.S. Army.

U.S. Senator John Slidell of Louisiana was the brother-in-law of Beauregard and used his influence to obtain the appointment for Beauregard as superintendent of West Point. He accepted the appointment but made it clear to the secretary of war that if Louisiana seceded, he would resign in favor of his home state.

Beauregard reported to his new post on January 23. On January 27, he received a telegram that his appointment was revoked. Unaware that Louisiana had seceded on January 26, Beauregard was furious over the revocation. He telegrammed Washington that "so long as I keep my opinions of the present unfortunate conditions of our country to myself, I most respectfully protest any act which might cast…reflection upon my reputation." He then received a telegram about the Louisiana secession, forwarded his written resignation to the secretary and left West Point.

When he arrived at the New York dock to catch a steamship to New Orleans, he discovered that the *Star of the West* was still docked at New York Harbor after its return from Charleston Harbor and the attack on Fort Morris. Captain McGowan invited Beauregard aboard, where he toured the ship and inspected the damage inflicted by The Citadel cadets.

On his return to New Orleans, Beauregard hoped to be named commander of the Louisiana State Army, an honor bestowed to Braxton Bragg instead. Bragg offered Beauregard a commission as colonel, but Beauregard would have no part of it. As an affront to Bragg, he enrolled as a private in the Orleans Guard, a battalion of Creole aristocrats.

Beauregard again used his connection to Senator Slidell, who spoke with newly elected Confederate President Jefferson Davis. On March 1, 1861, Davis appointed Beauregard to the rank of brigadier general in the Provisional Army of the Confederate States, making him the first appointment to general by the new president.

Davis then sent Beauregard to Charleston and Bragg to Pensacola, even though Bragg had served previously at Fort Moultrie and was very familiar with Charleston Harbor. It was Beauregard's expertise in artillery that swayed Davis, knowing that those skills would be in great need in Charleston.

Beauregard arrived in Charleston on March 3, 1861. Jefferson had high confidence in Beauregard, but he also appreciated that he was sending the Creole to face one of his mentors, Robert Anderson. In fact, Davis and Anderson were also close friends. Davis once referred to Anderson as "a true soldier and a man of the first sense of honor."

Anderson learned quickly that his good friend Beauregard had arrived to accept command. In a letter to Washington dated March 6, Anderson acknowledged, "The presence here, as commander, of General Beauregard, recently of the U.S. Engineers, insures, I think, in a great measure the exercise of skill and sound judgment in all operations of the South Carolinians in this harbor." He ended his letter with, "God grant that our country may be saved from the horrors of a fratricidal war!"

The stage was now set. Beauregard and Anderson—student and teacher, two experts in artillery, two men with great devotion to honor—now had the fate of a nation divided in their hands. Wigfall and other Confederate-friendly officials in Washington expected Lincoln to act quickly and advised Pickens accordingly. Wigfall cautioned Pickens to "be vigilant."

In a city typically slow to accept outsiders, Beauregard was received with open arms. He made his headquarters in a home at 37 Meeting

As long as mail service was allowed, Anderson and his engineer filed reports to Washington and watched the construction of the Confederate batteries around them. One officer mailed his sketch to *Harper's Weekly* of scenes viewed from Fort Sumter: Fort Johnson (bottom), Morris Island (middle) and Fort Moultrie (top).

Captain John Hamilton, CSN, developed the idea of a floating battery to be used in the assault on Fort Sumter. It was one hundred feet by twenty-five feet and was reinforced with two layers of railway iron on the front. The barge was armed with two forty-two-pound guns and two thirty-two-pound guns.

Street. He was as quick to insert himself in the social life of the city as he was the affairs of his military command. His olive complexion and trace of a French accent enthralled the ladies of Charleston, who frequently left flowers and gifts at his headquarters. He wrote Walker that he was "very well pleased with this place."

While the social life thrilled him, he was not so enamored with the defenses at Charleston. He began making changes immediately, preparing the city to defend an attack from the sea and, at the same time, place a ring of effective batteries around Fort Sumter. He used slave labor to build the batteries so that he could use the white men to drill and prepare them.

Walker agreed with Beauregard's rapid preparations. He assessed the situation in Charleston by pointing out, "Fort Sumter is silent now only because of the weakness of the garrison…If Sumter was properly garrisoned and armed, it would be a perfect Gibraltar to anything by constant shelling, night and day, from the four points on the compass. As it is, the weakness of the garrison constitutes our greatest advantage."

CHAPTER 11

A NEW PRESIDENT

On March 4, the day after Beauregard arrived in Charleston, Lincoln was inaugurated in Washington. In his inauguration speech, he stated: "I am loath to close. We are not enemies, but friends. We must not be enemies. Though passion may have strained, it must not break our bonds of affection. The mystic chords of memory, stretching from every battlefield, and patriot grave, to every living heart and hearthstone, all over this broad land, will yet swell the chorus of the Union, when again touched, as surely they will be, by the better angels of our nature."

After the inauguration, Buchanan rode with Lincoln back to the White House. Buchanan felt a great weight lifted from his shoulders. He was only too happy to pass the baton to Lincoln and walk away from the national crisis. As they entered the White House, Buchanan said to the new commander in chief, "My dear sir, if you are as happy in entering the White House as I shall feel on returning to Wheatland, you are a happy man indeed."

The text of Lincoln's inauguration speech was distributed across the country. No matter what one's inclination about the possibility of war, everyone, North and South, seemed to find contradictory meaning in the speech. Stephen Douglas, Lincoln's opponent in the November election, observed, "Well, I hardly know what he means. Every point in the address is susceptible of a double construction; but I think he does not mean coercion." Senator Wigfall disagreed with Douglas's interpretation. He wired to Pickens, "Inaugural means war."

The newspapers across the country were as contradictory. A Pittsburgh editorial declared that Lincoln's speech was "so clear, so simple, so direct." A Detroit newspaper called the speech "as clear as a mountain brook." The editor of the Raleigh, North Carolina paper wrote that Lincoln's message "was not a war message." The Knoxville, Tennessee paper declared that it was "a declaration of war against the seceded States!"

THE UNION IS DISSOLVED!

Abraham Lincoln was inaugurated as the sixteenth president of the United States on March 4, 1861.

Lincoln insisted that he had no desire to abolish slavery and "no lawful right to do so." He was clear, though, that he felt that secession was unconstitutional. He offered,

> *No government proper ever had a provision in its organic law for its own termination…Plainly, the central idea of secession is the essence of anarchy, the rule of minority, as a permanent arrangement, is wholly inadmissible…One section of our country believes slavery is right, and ought to be extended, while the other believes it is wrong, and ought not to be extended. This is the only dispute.*

Even though the Confederate States had formed, Ohio Congressman Thomas Corwin was still seeking a way to relieve the fears of the South regarding slavery. Though perhaps a last-ditch effort, Corwin proposed a constitutional amendment to forbid future attempts to amend the Constitution to "'abolish or interfere' with the 'domestic institutions' of the states, including 'persons held to labor or service.'" A similar version had been introduced in the Senate by Senator William Seward.

On February 28, the amendment passed the House of Representatives 133–65, one vote greater than the required two-thirds needed to approve. The Senate also passed the amendment two days later, 24–12, the exact margin needed to approve. There were no votes cast by the seven Southern states that had already seceded. President Buchanan publicly endorsed the amendment, hoping that it would ease the tensions in the country. Even Lincoln, in his inaugural address in March, did not oppose the amendment, stating, "Holding such a provision to now be implied Constitutional law, I have no objection to it being made express and irrevocable."

Interestingly, two states, Ohio and Maryland, did ratify the Corwin Amendment, but it moved no further. Since the amendment was not passed through Congress with a time limit, it is still technically before the states for approval.

Receiving the same warnings as Pickens, the Confederate War Department was expecting some movement by Lincoln. CSA Secretary of War Walker wrote Beauregard on March 9, informing the general that:

> *Fort Sumter is silent now only because of the weakness of the garrison. Should re-enforcements get in, her guns would open fire on you.*
>
> *There is information at this Department—not official, it is true, but believed to be reliable—that five or six United States ships are in New York Harbor all ready to start.*
>
> *The United States steamer "Pawnee" has left Philadelphia suddenly for Washington, fully provisioned and ready to go to sea, and it is probable that the effort to re-enforce Sumter may be made by sending in men in whale-boats.*

Just after the inauguration, the new rumor in Washington was that Lincoln would order Anderson to evacuate Fort Sumter, a choice favored by the newly appointed secretary of state, William Seward. Seward had worked hard behind the scenes to influence General Scott. On March 5, Scott wrote to Lincoln, expressing, "When Major Anderson first threw himself into Fort Sumter it would have been easy to reinforce him…The difficulty of reinforcing now has been increased 10 or 15 fold." Scott complained about Buchanan's indecision and the failure of Captain McGowan to reach Anderson in January as factors that had exacerbated the problem. "Evacuation seems almost inevitable…if indeed, the worn out garrison not be assaulted and carried in the present week."

The Union Is Dissolved!

On March 13, Captain Gustavus V. Fox, a former naval officer and trusted friend, met with President Lincoln to present a plan for a naval expedition to reinforce Fort Sumter. Lincoln received the plan as information but did not act on it. He did, however, send Fox to Charleston, where he met with Anderson. Anderson did not like the plan but did ask that Fox convey to the president that he would likely not be able to hold out past mid-April.

Anderson concurred with the written assessment of Captain Seymour, an officer in his command:

> *It is not more than possible to supply this fort by ruse with a few men or a small amount of provisions, such is the unceasing vigilance employed to prevent it. To do so openly by vessels alone, unless they are shot-proof, is virtually impossible, so numerous and powerful are the opposing batteries. No vessel can lay near the fort without being exposed to continual fire, and the harbor could, and probably would, whenever necessary, be effectually closed, as one channel has already been. A projected attack in large force would draw to this harbor all the available resources in men and material of the contiguous States. Batteries of heavy caliber would be multiplied rapidly and indefinitely. At least twenty thousand men, good marksmen and trained for months past with a view to this very contingency, would be concentrated here before the attacking force could leave Northern ports. The harbor could be closed. A landing must effected at some distance from our guns, which could give no aid. Charleston Harbor would be a Sebastopol in such a conflict, and unlimited means would probably be required to insure success, before which time the garrison of Fort Sumter would be starved out.*

CHAPTER 12

FRIENDS TO CHARLESTON

On March 21, Lincoln sent two close friends to Charleston: Ward Lamon and Stephen Hurlbut. Lamon was a former law partner with Lincoln in Illinois and currently served as a federal marshal in Washington. Hurlbut was also an Illinois attorney and was a Charleston native.

Lamon checked into the Charleston Hotel, where the custom was to write in your town of residence on the registration book. Lamon signed in immediately after a group of men from Virginia, allowing the perception that he was from Virginia as well.

He first called on James Petigru, the ardent Unionist in the city. Petigru took the meeting but advised Lamon that they not meet again "as every one who came near him was watched, and intercourse with him could only result in annoyance and danger to the visitor as well as to himself and would fail to promote any good to the Union cause." Shortly after this meeting, word got out in town that Lamon was not a Virginian but instead was a "Yankee Lincoln-hireling."

The next day, Lamon arranged to meet with Governor Pickens. As was his nature, Pickens was clear to Lamon, admonishing him that any attempt to reinforce Fort Sumter meant war. He reiterated that "nothing can prevent war except acquiescence of the President of the United States in secession, and his unalterable resolve not to attempt any reinforcements of the Southern forts." Lamon informed Pickens that no attempt to reinforce Anderson would occur and he ventured further, telling him that Fort Sumter would likely be abandoned.

Next, Lamon visited with Major Anderson at Fort Sumter. Anderson advised him that he was low on provisions, which consisted only of six barrels of flour, six barrels of hard bread, three barrels of sugar, one barrel of coffee, two barrels of vinegar, twenty-six barrels of pork, one quarter barrel of salt, one and a half barrels of rice and three boxes of candles.

Ward Lamon was a close personal friend and former law partner of Abraham Lincoln. *Courtesy of the Library of Congress.*

Stephen A. Hurlbut was born in Charleston. He was an officer of a South Carolina Infantry regiment in the Second Seminole War. *Courtesy of the Library of Congress.*

Charleston and Fort Sumter in the Civil War

By the time Lamon returned to the docks in Charleston, a large mob had formed. Fortunately for Lamon, former South Carolina Congressman Lawrence Keitt was nearby, and he whisked Lamon away. That night, Lamon boarded the train for Washington with Mr. and Mrs. Hurlbut.

He would later write that he was sent on a mission by the president to "the virtual capital of the state which had been the pioneer in all of this haughty and stupendous work of rebellion." He also expressed a concern over his safety while in Charleston, writing, "I was about to trust my precious life and limbs as a stranger within her gates and an enemy to her cause."

It has never been clear on what authority he left Pickens with the clear belief that Lincoln would withdraw from Fort Sumter. Lincoln himself had not expressed such an opinion, though that position was advanced passionately by Seward, in Lincoln's cabinet.

Hurlbut was in Charleston at the same time but was intentionally less visible than Lamon. Hurlbut's wife accompanied him on the trip, and they stayed with relatives in Charleston. He reported the sights in Charleston, writing:

> I rode around the City, visiting especially the wharves and the Battery so as to view the shipping in port and the Harbor. I regret to say that no single vessel in port displayed American Colours. Foreign craft had their National Colors; the Flag of the Southern Confederacy, and the State of South Carolina was visible everywhere—but the tall masts of Northern owned Ships were bare and showed no colors whatever. Four miles down the Harbor the Standard of the United States floated over Fort Sumter, the only evidence of jurisdiction and nationality.

Like Lamon, Hurlbut met with James Petigru. He also met with many businessmen and former acquaintances to gauge the depth of the sentiments in Charleston. He reported back to Lincoln:

> I have no hesitation in reporting as unquestionable, that Separate Nationality is a fixed fact, that there is an unanimity of sentiment which to my mind is astonishing—that there is no attachment to the Union—that almost every one of those very men who in 1832 held military commissions under secret orders from General Jackson and in fact were ready to draw the sword in civil war for the nation, are now as ready to take arms if necessary for the Southern Confederacy.

Hurlbut continued in noting that Charlestonians expected the city to, once again, become a center of financial influence resulting from secession.

"They expect a Golden age," he reported, "when Charleston shall be a great Commercial Emporium and Control for the South as New York does for the North." He advised Lincoln that any ship attempting to transport provisions to Fort Sumter would be stopped and that abandoning the post in Charleston Harbor would harm the current administration here and abroad.

After Lamon's statements that Lincoln would withdraw Anderson from Fort Sumter, authorities in Charleston became more confident that they could negotiate a resolution to this stalemate. On one evening, Episcopal priest Reverend A. Toomer Porter encountered Colonel James Chestnut at the Battery:

> *I remarked to him, "These are troubled times, Colonel; we are at the beginning of a terrible war." "Not at all," he said. "There will be no war, it will all be arranged. I will drink all the blood shed in the war." So little did some of our leaders realize the awful import of what we were doing.*

Lincoln was in a classic no-win situation. Reinforcing Anderson was not likely without incurring much damage and loss of life. Withdrawing Anderson would forever damage the image of his new administration and most certainly weaken the Union. One Republican remarked to Lincoln, "I tell you, sir, if Fort Sumter is evacuated, the new administration is done forever." Another politician pontificated, "Lincoln is like an ass between two stacks of hay."

As Lamon reported back to Lincoln regarding Anderson's shrinking supply of provisions, Beauregard was reporting to Montgomery that he was within two to three days of completing his artillery preparations across the harbor of Charleston.

Based upon Lamon's meeting with Pickens, Beauregard wrote Anderson on March 26 that he understood that "yourself and command would be transferred to another post in a few days." He assured Anderson that if Washington would withdraw the garrison, he had no intention of dishonoring him by asking for a formal surrender. He continued, assuring Anderson:

> *We will be happy to see that you are provided with proper means of transportation out of this harbor for yourself and command, including baggage, private and company property. All that will be required of you on account of the public rumors that have reached us will be your word of honor as an officer and a gentleman, that the fort, all public property therein, its armament, etc., shall remain in their present condition...On our part no objection will be raised to your retiring with your side and company arms, and to your saluting your flag on lowering it.*

Though Beauregard was anxious to seize this moment of attention and responsibility with his new command, he also had misgivings about facing his old mentor, now penned in at Fort Sumter. As a gesture of friendship and respect, on one occasion, Beauregard sent several cases of fine brandy and several boxes of cigars to Anderson. Anderson, not anxious to fraternize with Beauregard, responded that he only required the necessary provisions for his command to fulfill its duty.

Frustration was mounting in Washington. While everyone expected quick action from the new administration, four weeks had now passed and everything was status quo. Massachusetts Congressman Charles Francis Adams, the son of former President John Quincy Adams, remarked, "The impression which I have received is that the course of the President is drifting the country into war, by want of decision. For my part I see nothing but incompetency in the head. The man is not equal to the hour." A prominent Wisconsin politician, Carl Schurz, wrote to Lincoln expressing his concerns: "Everybody asks: what is the policy of the Administration? And everybody replies: Any distinct line of policy, be it war or a recognition of the Southern Confederacy, would be better than this uncertain state of things."

The House of Representatives, in debate, expressed its concern over the inaction of the Lincoln administration.

The Union Is Dissolved!

On March 29, Lincoln met with his cabinet to once again hear any opinions about an effective strategy regarding Fort Sumter. As had been the case from the beginning, the members of the cabinet were deeply divided in their opinions as to a logical course of action. Seward asserted, "I do not think it wise to provoke a Civil War beginning at Charleston in rescue of an untenable position." In truth, Lincoln had already made up his mind to send a naval expedition, though he kept his decision from even the secretary of war and the secretary of the navy.

The fact that Lincoln chose his own path came as no surprise to some. William Henry Herndon, a former law partner of Lincoln's, spoke of his associate: "He was the most secretive—reticent—shut-mouthed man that ever lived. He was so stubborn that nothing could penetrate his mind once he had made a decision."

Chapter 13

"A Sheep Tied"

Anderson, penned up now in Fort Sumter, expressed that he felt like he was "a sheep tied, watching the butcher sharpening a knife to cut his throat." By April, Anderson was growing restless in Fort Sumter with an endless stalemate at hand. He remarked, "I must say that I think the Government has left me too much to myself—has not given me instructions, even when I asked for them." Despite his misgivings, he was steadfast in his determination, often insisting, "That flag which has been raised with prayer, shall never be lowered except with honor."

The workmen, who had been at Fort Sumter since December, had completed all that could be accomplished in the isolated fort. When Anderson requested permission to send them ashore, Montgomery instructed Beauregard, "No portion of the garrison must be permitted to leave unless all go."

In Washington, Chief of Engineers Joseph Totten wrote to the secretary of war, obviously frustrated. He insisted that disaster could only be averted "by sending a large army and navy to capture all the surrounding forts and batteries," but he added that there was no time for such a complicated expedition. He ended by recognizing, "If we do not evacuate Fort Sumter it will be wrested from us by force."

On April 4, Lincoln met with Captain Fox to accept his proposal for a naval expedition to travel to Charleston. However, the president was clear that Anderson would be notified and even Governor Pickens would receive advance notice.

The notice to Anderson was written by the president but signed by Simon Cameron, secretary of war. It read:

Sir: Your letter of the 1ˢᵗ instant occasions some anxiety to the President.

On the information of Captain Fox he had supposed you could hold out till the 15ᵗʰ instant without any great inconvenience; and had prepared an expedition to relieve you before that period.

Hoping that you will be able to sustain yourself till the 11ᵗʰ or 12ᵗʰ instant, the expedition will go forward; and, finding your flag flying, will attempt to provision you, and, in case the effort is resisted, will endeavor also to reinforce you.

You will therefore hold out, if possible, till the arrival of the expedition.

It is not, however, the intention of the President to subject your command to any danger or hardship beyond what, in your judgment, would be usual in military life; and he has entire confidence that you will act as becomes a patriot and soldier, under the circumstances.

Whenever, if at all, in your judgment, to save yourself and command, a capitulation becomes a necessity, you are authorized to make it.

On April 6, President Lincoln penned an unsigned, unaddressed message to Governor Pickens and sent it for personal delivery by Robert Chew, a trusted State Department clerk. The note read:

I am directed by the President of the United States to notify you to expect an attempt will be made to supply Fort Sumter with provisions only; and that, if such an attempt be not resisted, no effort to throw in men, arms, or ammunition will be made without further notice, or in case of an attack by upon the fort.

Whether it was intentional or not, Lincoln's message was strategically ambiguous. It was unclear whether Lincoln would choose to use force in Charleston.

The ships were assembled in New York by Fox to sail to Fort Sumter. The most powerful ship of the group, the USS *Powhatan*, left the harbor prematurely and with a captain different from the orders dispatched to New York. The *Powhatan* was a side-wheel steam frigate, the largest of the navy's paddle frigates. It was armed with one eleven-inch Dahlgren gun, ten nine-inch Dahlgren guns and five twelve-pound guns.

The published orders assigned Captain Mercer to command the *Powhatan*; however, before the change of command could take place, Lieutenant David Porter left New York commanding the warship. When a smaller ship caught up to the *Powhatan*, Porter responded that he was under secret, sealed orders directly from Lincoln. Whether Lincoln actually ordered the ship to sail or it was Seward using Lincoln's name was never known, but the *Powhatan* was not heading to Fort Sumter—it was sailing to Fort Pickens in Florida.

The loss of the powerful *Powhatan* seriously compromised the prospects for Fox's expedition. The USS *Pawnee*, USS *Pocahontas*, USS *Harriet Lane* and two transports under the command of Captain Fox did set sail for Charleston. On April 6, authorities in Charleston received a telegram from Washington simply signed "A Friend." It read, "Positively determined not to withdraw Anderson. Supplies go immediately, supported by a naval force under Stringham if their landing is resisted."

The next day, Beauregard stopped all supply deliveries and mail service for Fort Sumter. At the post office, officers seized two official letters from Sumter, one written by Anderson and the other by Foster. Opening the Anderson report, Beauregard and Pickens were surprised to learn that supplies at the fort were extremely low. Anderson also indicated that based on Lamon's remarks in March, he was shocked to hear that an expedition was now en route. Anderson expressed, "We shall strive to do our duty, though I frankly say that my heart is not in this war which I see is to be thus commenced."

Beauregard notified Anderson, "I have the honor to inform you that, in consequence of the delays and apparent vacillations of the United States Government at Washington relative to the evacuation of Fort Sumter, no further communications…will be permitted." Even though the mail had now stopped, Anderson continued writing daily reports that he would deliver when he could.

The letter from Lincoln to Pickens was forwarded to the Confederate government in Montgomery. Confederate Secretary of War Walker sent a telegram to Beauregard with simple instructions: "Under no circumstance are you to allow provisions to be sent to Fort Sumter." On April 10, President Davis wired Beauregard to demand the evacuation of the fort and to attack it if refused. Not everyone in the Confederate government was resolved to start the war. Secretary of State Robert Toombs argued that firing on Fort Sumter "will inaugurate a civil war greater than any the world has yet seen…It is suicide, murder, and will lose us every friend at the North. You will wantonly strike a hornet's nest which extends from mountains to ocean, and legions now quiet will swarm out and sting us to death. It is unnecessary; it puts us in the wrong; it is fatal."

Later the same day, Beauregard received a shipment of powder from Augusta. This shipment completed the necessary supplies to initiate the conflict. Beauregard wired Walker that his demand for Anderson's surrender "will be made to-morrow at 12 o'clock." The Confederate government was determined to force Anderson's hand before the arrival of the New York expedition.

During the four-month standoff at Fort Sumter, Charlestonians gathered daily at the Battery to gaze onto the island fort holding the defiant Federal garrison.

This engraving of Charleston that appeared in *Harper's Weekly* was sketched from the steeple of St. Michael's Church looking east down Broad Street.

Charleston and Fort Sumter in the Civil War

Concerned that the Federal troops on the way might land on Morris Island to gain control of that flank, Beauregard placed two thousand there. An additional six thousand troops surrounded Fort Sumter in a circle of fire.

Private Thompson, stationed with Anderson at Fort Sumter, recorded:

> Our supply of breadstuffs was fast giving out, and the Carolinians knew it. They had cut off all communication with the shore, and starvation was staring us in the face. We had been on ¾ rations for a long time and on the 8ᵗʰ of April a reduction to half rations was made and cheerfully submitted to, the hope of being re-enforced or withdrawn having not yet entirely left us. On the eleventh one biscuit was our allowance, and matters seemed rapidly coming to a crisis.

Even the *Charleston Courier*, typically much more moderate than the *Mercury*, wrote in an editorial on April 11, "We are sick of the subject of evacuation… Let the strife begin." News reached Charleston the same morning that the naval expedition led by Captain Fox was not far away.

That afternoon, Beauregard sent Colonel James Chesnut Jr. and Captain Stephen Dill Lee to Fort Sumter to deliver a message. The letter delivered an ultimatum to Anderson:

> I am ordered by the Government of the Confederate States to demand the evacuation of Fort Sumter. My aides, Colonel Chestnut and Captain Lee, are authorized to make such demand of you. All proper facilities will be afforded for the removal of yourself and command, together with company arms and property, and all private property, to any post in the United States which you may select. The flag which you have upheld so long and with so much fortitude, under the most trying circumstances, may be saluted by you on taking it down.

Anderson conferred with his officers and penned a reply to his former protégé:

> General: I have the honor to acknowledge the receipt of your communication demanding the evacuation of this fort, and to say, in reply thereto, that it is a demand with which I regret that my sense of honor, and of my obligations to my Government, prevent my compliance. Thanking you for the fair, manly and courteous terms proposed, and for the high compliment paid me, I am, very respectfully,

THE UNION IS DISSOLVED!

Your Obedient Servant,
Robert Anderson, Major, First Artillery, Commanding

Anderson presented the letter to Chesnut and Lee and walked them to their boat. In conversation, Anderson informed them, "I will await the first shot, and if you do not batter us to pieces we will be starved out in a few days." Beauregard wired all of this information to Walker in Montgomery.

Citadel superintendent Peter Stevens was stationed on Morris Island. Word had reached his camp that the demand for surrender had been presented to Anderson. As he looked out on Fort Sumter, he saw the United States flag flying above the fort split in two. He remarked to his men, "I wonder if that is emblematical?" The flag remained torn for several minutes before being replaced by a new one. The men on Morris Island all agreed that it was a good omen.

Walker responded that if Anderson would set a time to evacuate and agree not to use his guns, Beauregard could negotiate the peaceful taking of the fort. Shortly thereafter, Beauregard received a wire from friends in Washington indicating that an article in the *Tribune* stated that the expedition en route to Charleston would arrive to relieve Anderson and "that a force will be landed which will overcome all opposition."

On the night of April 11, lookouts spotted the masts of the Federal ships forming offshore. Anderson sent word to Beauregard that he would agree to evacuate the fort on April 15, provided that he received no further instructions or supplies from Washington. With the relief expedition already offshore from Charleston, Beauregard dared not wait. At 3:20 a.m. on Friday, April 12, he sent word to Anderson, once again by Chesnut and Lee, that he "will open fire of his batteries on Fort Sumter in one hour from this time." Anderson responded to them, "If we never meet in this world again, God grant that we may meet in the next."

CHAPTER 14

THE FIRST SHOT

Chesnut and Lee left Fort Sumter and retired to Fort Johnson. It was agreed that a mortar from Fort Johnson would fire a shot over Fort Sumter as the signal for all batteries to open fire. There were two batteries constructed at Fort Johnson: one was near the beach facing Fort Sumter and the other, referred to as the Hill Battery, was near the summer village used by the James Island planters. They would need to tear down one of the cottages for the Hill Battery to have a clear shot at Sumter. Instead, Chesnut and Captain George S. James agreed that the beach battery would fire the opening signal shot.

James offered the honor to Roger Pryor, a former congressman from Virginia. Prior had resigned his seat just a month before, and even though Virginia had not yet seceded from the Union, he went to Charleston to play a role in the confrontation. The opportunity to fire the first shot left the Virginian emotionally overwhelmed. He looked at James and responded, "I could not fire the first gun of the war." He got into a boat with three aides and started rowing to Charleston at 4:15 a.m.

At many of the large homes on the Battery, house slaves had organized carpets and set out chairs and tables on the flat rooftops so that their masters and invited guests could watch the pending bombardment. The streets below filled with people looking for a good vantage point to watch the action. Some children climbed the tall lanterns on the Battery to peer out to the small island where Fort Sumter was perched.

Chesnut ordered James to fire the signal shot at precisely 4:30 a.m. Lieutenant Henry S. Farley, commander of the beach battery, readied the mortar and held the lanyard waiting for the signal. At exactly 4:30 a.m., James gave the order; Farley pulled the lanyard and fired the signal shot. The shell fired through the early morning air on a perfect trajectory and exploded

THE UNION IS DISSOLVED!

After all negotiations had failed, the first shot to signal the attack on Fort Sumter was fired from a battery at Fort Johnson. By 5:00 a.m. on April 12, Fort Sumter was taking on fire from all the Confederate batteries in the harbor.

right over Fort Sumter. The second shot, also from Fort Johnson, was fired by Lieutenant W.H. Gibbes of Columbia. (The wood used in the construction of the magazine was saved by Dr. Robert Lebby and used to build several pieces of furniture that have been passed through the generations of several James Island families.)

On Morris Island, the avowed secessionist from Virginia, Edmund Ruffin, pulled the lanyard of a Columbiad at the Iron Battery on Cummings Point. The shot hit the parapet of Fort Sumter and lodged in the wall about one foot from the head of Captain Doubleday.

By 5:00 a.m., guns from two batteries on James Island, Cummings Point on Morris Island, a battery in Mount Pleasant and four batteries on Sullivan's Island were firing on Fort Sumter. Mary Chesnut, the wife of Colonel James Chesnut, was asleep in Charleston when she was startled awake by the booming of the guns. She recorded in her diary, "I sprang out of my bed, and on my knees prostrate, I prayed as I never prayed before."

The ever vigilant *Mercury* covered the firing on Fort Sumter:

> *As may have been anticipated from the notice of the military movements in our city yesterday, the bombardment of Fort Sumter, so long and anxiously*

Edmund Ruffin, angry that Virginia was not the first state to secede, left his home state for South Carolina. *Courtesy of the Library of Congress.*

This engraving appeared on the cover of *Harper's Weekly* announcing the commencement of the Confederate attack on Fort Sumter. This scene, however, was drawn in New York since Charleston refused to allow *Harper's* correspondents into the city after Lincoln's election.

expected, has at length become a fact accomplished. The restless activity of the night before was gradually worn down, the citizens who had thronged the Battery through the night, anxious and weary, had sought their homes, the Mounted Guard which had kept watch and ward over the city, with the first grey streak of morning were preparing to retire, when two guns in quick succession from Fort Johnson announced the opening of the drama.

Upon that signal, the circle of batteries with which the grim fortress of Fort Sumter is beleaguered opened fire. The outline of this great volcanic crater was illuminated with a line of twinkling lights; the clustering shells illuminated the sky above it; the balls clattering thick as hail upon its sides; our citizens, roused to a forgetfulness of their fatigue through many weary hours, rushed again to the points of observation; and so, at the break of day, amidst the bursting of bombs, the roaring of ordnance, and before thousands of spectators, whose homes, and liberties, and lives were all at stake, was enacted the first great scene in the opening drama of what, it is presumed, will be a most momentous military act.

Beauregard was precise in his orders about the firing on Fort Sumter. The forty-three guns at the Confederate batteries were instructed to fire in order, in a counterclockwise circle around the harbor, with exactly two minutes in between each shot. This rhythm gave him enough munitions to maintain a steady fire for forty-eight hours. However, with the excitement and adrenaline of the inexperienced gunners, they quickly fell out of order and the guns trained on Sumter would simply repeat their fire as the guns were ready.

Even in the morning fog, the many spectators circled around the harbor could see the flight of the shells shrieking toward Fort Sumter. Though more than three miles away, the concussion of shells hitting Sumter's walls was felt in the homes downtown. The booming sounds of the guns could be heard more than forty miles away.

Planters and their families in Upper St. John's Parish boarded the morning train to Charleston to view the excitement, even as the trains were already filled with soldiers also heading to Charleston.

Anderson did not return fire for several hours. His larger guns were on the top tiers of the fort, and in order to fire them, his men would have to expose themselves and potentially incur heavy casualties, which would devastate a garrison already too small. He chose instead to man the smaller guns in the lowest tier of the fort. However, these thirty-two- and forty-two-pound guns would do little damage firing onto the ironclad Confederate batteries, sand batteries and the walls of Fort Moultrie, protected by cotton bales.

Anderson also favored the lower-tier guns since they would be more effective in the event of a Confederate attempt to storm the fort to overwhelm the small garrison. When Anderson did not immediately return fire, Beauregard was agitated. He felt that if Anderson did not return fire it "would have cheapened our conquest of the fort."

Anderson tried to keep his men calm after the firing commenced. Just after 6:00 a.m., roll call was taken. The men, as usual, were sent to breakfast. Their morning consisted of what they had on hand—old salt pork. The officers dined in their mess as shot and shell fell over Sumter. Doubleday later wrote, "We had retained one colored man to wait on us. He was a spruce looking mulatto from Charleston, very active and efficient on culinary occasions." Doubleday noted that he was "completely demoralized by the thunder of the guns and crashing of the shot around us. He leaned back against the wall, almost white with fear, his eyes closed, and his whole expression was one of personal despair."

After breakfast, the Federal troops were divided into groups and assigned to guns. Musicians and workmen were assigned to assist gun crews. Doubleday commanded one company and Seymour the other, working in alternating shifts. By 6:30 a.m., Fort Sumter began to return fire. Like the Confederates, the Federal troops were excitedly firing in quick repetition. At that rate, Anderson calculated that they could be out of cartridges by late afternoon, and therefore defenseless. Accordingly, Anderson restricted the men to firing no more than six guns at a time.

Anderson and the officers realized that among their other problems of too few men and gun cartridges, their greatest liability was the threat of fire. The fort's exterior walls, made of brick and rock, were fireproof, but the interior buildings in the fort were made of wood. These buildings contained the stairwells to move from tier to tier and the ammunition storage. If the Confederates fired hot-shot, and he knew they would, these buildings would incinerate. On the first day alone, three sizable fires broke out, giving the garrison a greater threat, perhaps, than the Confederate batteries pounding the fort.

The soldiers in Sumter quickly grew tired and agitated with the incessant bombardment. Soldiers on the northern side of Sumter grew annoyed at the crowd of civilians gathered in front of the Moultrie House on Sullivan's Island. Two sergeants, without permission, fired onto the spectators, missing them but hitting the second floor of the hotel.

As predicted, the Confederate batteries did begin firing hot-shot. Hot-shot was solid iron balls that were preheated in a furnace and fired. If it was fired onto a wooden ship or, in this case, the wooden structures in Fort Sumter, the solid balls would strike and sit smoldering until the wood was ignited.

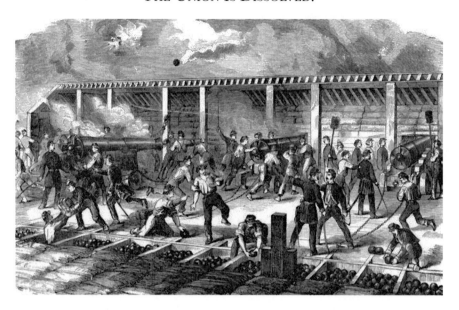

Though the "floating battery" was anchored, it was most effective in the attack on Fort Sumter. As designed, the iron-front face on the battery took several direct hits but sustained no real damage.

This engraving published in the *Illustrated London News* is from April 12, as the guns in the lower tier of Fort Sumter were firing on Fort Moultrie.

Charleston and Fort Sumter in the Civil War

In his report to Confederate authorities in Montgomery, Beauregard offered, "During the day the fire of my batteries was kept up most spiritedly, the guns and mortars being worked in the coolest manner, preserving the prescribed intervals of firing. Towards the evening it became evident that our fire was very effective."

The Federal ships had, in fact, begun arriving off the coast of Charleston. The *Harriet Lane* arrived first, the day before. Next, the unarmed *Baltic*, with Captain Fox aboard, rendezvoused with the first ship at 3:00 a.m. on April 12. The *Pawnee* arrived after dawn, after firing had already started. The *Pocahontas* had not arrived and Captain Stephen Rowan did not want to move to the harbor channel without the firepower of the *Powhatan*. Of course, his wait would be eternal, since the *Powhatan* was not sailing to Charleston, as they thought—it was heading to Florida.

The ship's commanders finally agreed to move the *Harriet Lane* and the *Pawnee* to the mouth of the harbor, but the *Baltic* would remain at the rendezvous point looking for the other ships. Private Thompson at Fort Sumter wrote,

> *Towards mid-day we could distinctly see a fleet of three war vessels off the bay, and we were certain they were an expedition fitted out to relieve us, and the hopes of speedily getting assistance compensated for the lack of anything in the shape of dinner…We confidently expected the fleet to make some attempt to land supplies and re-enforcements during the night, it being dark as pitch and raining, but we were disappointed. Morning dawned and with appetites unappeased and haggard look, although determined and confident, all took their positions for the day's work.*

The Confederates on Morris Island carefully watched the movement of the Federal ships. They fully expected troops from those ships to attempt a landing on Morris Island using small boats, possibly around 7:00 p.m., when the tide would be highest. The landing, however, never materialized.

As nightfall came around 7:00 p.m., Anderson had his men cease fire to conserve rounds. They settled to a meal of rancid pork and went to work sewing more gun cartridges for Saturday. The sentries posted were on the lookout for both Confederates attempting a landing at Fort Sumter or compatriots from the Federal fleet to resupply them. Through the night, neither occurred.

The Confederate guns calmed as well during the night, though Beauregard ordered that two batteries of mortars maintain a rhythm of firing every fifteen minutes to unsettle the Federal garrison. Anderson had several officers inspect the fort, and while the brick walls had received many direct hits, the damage was still superficial at this point. He had incurred no loss of life in his garrison, but four men were injured. The strategy of keeping his men below paid off.

During the rainy night, a number of commercial vessels arrived at Charleston Harbor. Seeing the mortar fire, they elected not to attempt an entry to the shipping channel, concerned that they would be viewed as a threat. Keeping watch on the Federal ships at night, sentries on Morris Island could see through the sea lightning that the number of ships was increasing. They assumed the worst—that these new arrivals were warships. With the heavy rain and strong seas, they were not as concerned that a landing would be attempted in the night.

Fox was on the *Pawnee* and was angry that the *Powhatan* and *Pocahontas* had not arrived. Without those two warships, he lacked the firepower to mount a naval attack. He considered sending in supplies by small boats, but the *Harriet Lane* had no such boats and the *Pawnee* only one. Fox transferred to the *Baltic* to look for the missing warships, but to no avail. Still frustrated, Fox tried to convince Captains Rowan and France to attempt to resupply Anderson, but neither would agree to tackle the rough seas at night.

After the firing on Fort Sumter, the *New York Herald* stated in an editorial, "Oceans of blood and millions of treasure will be wasted, with no other imaginable end than to leave the country exhausted, impoverished and wretched, and worse than all, despoiled of the freedom purchased at such cost by our forefathers."

On Saturday, April 13, the Confederate guns began firing again just after daybreak. Like the day before, Anderson had his men stay below to eat their breakfast of pork. With the small number of cartridges available to him, Anderson instructed his men to fire only on Sullivan's Island and fire slowly.

At 7:30 a.m., a Confederate shell landed on the officers' quarters in Fort Sumter, causing a fire. By 8:00 a.m., everyone across the harbor could see the thick, black smoke rising from Fort Sumter. As the blaze increased, the Confederate batteries kept pounding the beleaguered fort.

The Federal ships on the bar could see the fire as well, burning out of control. Commander Rowan of the *Pawnee* and Captain Fox felt compelled to help in some way but had few options. Finally, by noon, Rowan decided to seize one of the civilian ships waiting with them on the bar. He picked a schooner and fired a warning, causing its captain to come about. The ship was delivering a load of ice from Boston to Charleston.

Rowan planned to use the ice schooner to load supplies and recruits to send to Fort Sumter after dark. Fox figured that the ship would never get past the many batteries, but he agreed to the plan. At 2:00 p.m., the *Pocahontas* finally arrived. While this bolstered their force, it was the *Powhatan* that was needed the most. It not only had the firepower needed, but it was also outfitted with fighting launches and carried three hundred sailors.

All day Saturday, people crowded on the Battery and the docks and mounted the steeples and rooftops to watch the battle. Pickens was jubilant. He wired Governor Letcher in Virginia, "We can sink the fleet if they attempt to enter the channel. If they land elsewhere we can whip them...The war is commenced, and we will triumph or perish." A teacher, Anna Brackett, was among the large crowd of spectators. She wrote, "Women of all ages and ranks of life look eagerly out with spyglasses and opera glasses. Children talk and laugh and walk back and forth in the small moving space as if they were at a public show."

While the fire continued to rage in the fort, Anderson grew concerned about the three hundred barrels of gunpowder remaining. Although it was stored in a magazine, loose gunpowder was ever-present throughout the fort. The troops started moving the gunpowder and covered the barrels with wet blankets. After fewer than one hundred barrels had been moved, the fire was getting too close to the magazine, and Anderson ordered the thick metal doors closed and the entrance covered with dirt.

The firing onto Fort Sumter was intense, continuing for thirty-six hours before Anderson finally raised a white flag.

After the barracks and hospital at Fort Sumter caught fire, flames eventually approached the powder magazine. The Union troops were only able to remove one-third of the powder before the out-of-control fire posed too large of a threat. The magazine was then closed and the entrance was covered with dirt.

During the peak of the attack, the garrison flag was shot down. Confederate observers thought, initially, that Anderson was signaling his capitulation. Those thoughts were dashed, as Peter Hart seized the flag and nailed it to the highest point of the wall still standing at Fort Sumter.

As the fire continued to move and threaten the barrels covered in blankets, he ordered that all the barrels except four be thrown over the walls of the fort to the sea to lessen the danger. Some of the barrels got hung up on the rocks and did not roll to the water. Finally, a Confederate shell hit them, causing an enormous explosion.

Fire finally reached a stairwell containing several hundred nine-inch grenades, causing them to explode. The thick smoke became the greatest enemy to the Federal troops, choking them. All the men covered their faces with wet handkerchiefs. Others collapsed to the ground to avoid what they could of the thick, black smoke.

When Charlestonians saw the fort become devoured in fire, the reactions were mixed. At the Battery a boy shouted, "Now you'll see that old flag go down." A woman in the crowd exclaimed, "We forgot our people, we forgot everything, for a few moments, but the gallant band within the burning crater." Even the grizzled secessionist Edmund Ruffin expressed his concern: "I looked on with my feelings of joy and exultation at our now certain prospect of speedy success mixed with awe and horror of the danger of this terrible calamity, and pity for the men exposed to the consequences—and with high admiration for the indomitable spirit of the brave commander."

During the fight, Fort Sumter's flagstaff was hit seven times during the day. When it finally fell, the Confederates and spectators around the harbor immediately wondered if Anderson had relented and lowered his flag. For a moment, the Federal guns paused. Police Sergeant Peter Hart nailed the flag to a temporary flagstaff and nailed it to the highest point of the wall remaining. With the colors once again flying, the Federal fire resumed and the Confederates surrounding the fort cheered the struggling garrison for not quitting.

Hart, the hero of the moment, was never intended to be at Fort Sumter. In December, when Anderson had moved his garrison to Fort Sumter, Eba Anderson, an invalid at this point in her life, was in New York. Against doctor's orders, she was determined to see her husband in South Carolina. She located Hart, who had served with Anderson in Mexico, and asked him to accompany her for the journey. When Hart and Eba Anderson arrived in Charleston, Pickens had already restricted access. He relented to Mrs. Anderson's pleas provided that Hart pledge not to take up arms. A man of honor, Hart never did, but he decided to stay behind to support his former commander and the troops.

CHAPTER 15

BLOODLESS VICTORY

Colonel Wigfall, on his own initiative, took a boat from Cummings Point to Fort Sumter when the garrison flag fell. Even though the flag was replaced while he was en route, he continued on to speak with Anderson. He arrived at the fort while it was still under fire and was greeted by Foster, Meade and Davis. Wigfall told them, "Your flag is down, you are on fire, and you are not firing your guns. General Beauregard wants you to stop this." Truthfully, Wigfall had not spoken to Beauregard and the general had not sent him to the fort.

The three officers sent for Anderson. When he arrived, Wigfall said, "You have defended your flag nobly, Sir. You have done all that is possible to do, and General Beauregard wants to stop this fight. On what terms will you evacuate this fort?" Anderson was pleased that Wigfall strategically used the term "evacuate" rather than "surrender." The Federal major indicated that he had already presented his terms to Beauregard days earlier, but that he would evacuate right away rather than wait until April 15. Wigfall agreed to the terms and left to communicate this to Beauregard. Anderson then ordered the garrison flag down and a white bed sheet raised to stop the hostilities.

Wigfall left in his boat to Morris Island. Seeing the white bed sheet over the fort, the Confederates were already cheering the former senator. Wigfall stood in his boat waving his flag, shouting, "Sumter is ours!"

Before Wigfall had even departed the fort, Beauregard's actual emissaries were en route to Fort Sumter. In the boat were Stephen Dill Lee, Porcher Miles and Roger Pryor. When they arrived at the fort, they offered Beauregard's assistance with the fire. The three men were bewildered to hear that Anderson had already conveyed his agreement to evacuate. The men indicated that they were not authorized to offer terms and would have to confer with General

Beauregard. This agitated Anderson, and he suggested that they withdraw and he would raise his flag and resume firing. After speaking with one another privately, they asked Anderson to write down the exact terms agreed to with Wigfall and they would take them to Beauregard for consideration.

While the conversation was taking place, Pryor, who was thirsty, spotted a bottle of liquid nearby and took a big sip. He had taken a large gulp of iodide of potassium that belonged to the garrison surgeon, Dr. Crawford. Help was called for, and Dr. Crawford appeared and informed Pryor that he had poisoned himself. Crawford ran to the dispensary, located a stomach pump and hurried back to Pryor to relieve him.

While the other officers and Anderson were waiting on Pryor to recover, Anderson asked the Confederates about any injuries. They responded that several men had been wounded but they had no reports of loss of life. Anderson responded, "Thank God…There has been a higher power over us." The fact that no soldier on either side was killed was incredible, given that the Confederate batteries had fired more than 3,300 shots and Fort Sumter had returned with 1,000 shots.

Before Lee, Miles and Pryor could depart, two more Beauregard aides arrived. They indicated that Beauregard would accept the previous terms discussed on April 11 but the garrison could not salute its flag. Anderson sent the five aides back to town, agreeing to the terms, but he noted that he would appreciate Beauregard's consideration of allowing them to salute the Stars and Stripes on their exit.

Just before 6:00 p.m., Beauregard sent a message to Fort Sumter in response:

> On being informed that you were in distress, caused by a conflagration in Fort Sumter, I immediately dispatched my aides Colonels Miles and Pryor, and Captain Lee, to offer you any assistance in my power to give.
>
> Learning a few minutes afterwards that a white flag was waving on your ramparts, I sent two others of my aides, Colonel Allston and Major Jones, to offer you the following terms of evacuation: All proper facilities for the removal of yourself and command, together with company arms and private property, to any point within the United States you may select.
>
> Apprised that you desire the privilege of saluting your flag on retiring, I cheerfully concede it, in consideration of the gallantry with which you have defended the place under your charge.
>
> The Catawba steamer will be at the landing to-morrow morning at any hour you may designate for the purpose of transporting you whither you may desire.

Anderson acknowledged receipt of Beauregard's letter and asked that the *Catawba* be at Fort Sumter at 9:00 a.m.

News of the surrender was received in Charleston with great celebration. Bonfires and fireworks illuminated the night sky in the city. One woman exclaimed, "Wonderful, miraculous, unheard of in history, a bloodless victory." Charlestonian Henry William Ravenel pondered, "The first act in the drama is over! Will it end thus, or is it only the opening of a bloody tragedy?" Some of the officers in Charleston still expected the naval expedition to send troops to Morris Island despite Anderson's surrender.

As the men of the garrison in Fort Sumter looked out at the naval expedition still sitting at the bar, their anger was understandable. They still did not realize that most of the ships they could see were commercial steamers, not naval vessels. Fox sent a messenger to the Confederates to inquire about the white flag at Sumter. General Simons revealed to him that Anderson had surrendered. The messenger asked if the *Pawnee* could come

At 1:30 p.m. on Saturday, April 13, Anderson ordered the garrison flag to be lowered and a bed sheet was raised to indicate his surrender. Celebrations broke out throughout the city of Charleston.

in under a flag of truce to remove the garrison. When told no, he asked if the *Baltic*, an unarmed merchant steamer, could come in. Simons indicated that he would ask that of Beauregard.

Onboard the *Baltic*, Captain Fox was enraged when he saw the white flag extend above the walls of Sumter. His plan was all for naught—the fort surrendered before he could act. He was still fuming over the continued absence of the *Powhatan*. His ship that was meant to rescue the abandoned garrison would, instead, evacuate them. Before the messenger left, Simons asked the officer for his guarantee that the fleet would not attempt an attack. The lieutenant insisted that they would not.

Beauregard wired the great news to Secretary of War Walker. In his response, Walker had already turned his attention to the next challenge, stating, "Accept my congratulations. You have won your spurs. How many guns can you spare for Pensacola?"

On Sunday morning, Confederate Captain Hartstene arrived at Fort Sumter before dawn. He was to take one of Anderson's officers to meet with the fleet to make transportation arrangements. Hartstene indicated that the steamer *Isabel* would pick them up and transport them to the Federal ships at the bar. Anderson agreed, and then Hartstene handed him a mailbag with letters and reports that had accumulated over the last six days.

In Charleston, the governor declared Sunday to be "A Day of National Fasting, Thanksgiving, and Prayer." Many families arrived by boat to the harbor to watch the United States flag be retired and the raising of the South Carolina and Confederate flags.

By late morning, the *Isabel* anchored just off from Fort Sumter. The water was shallow and small boats were used to transport property to the steamship. At 12:15 p.m., Pickens and his wife, with Jamison, Magrath, Chesnut, Manning, Miles, Pryor and others, watched the transfer of the fort to the Confederates. As they approached the fort, it was obvious that the transfer was not yet ready and they landed at Sullivan's Island instead.

In the fort, Anderson presented the keys to Fort Sumter to Beauregard's aide, Captain Sam Ferguson, who was accompanied by a company of the Palmetto Guard. Ruffin entered with them carrying their flag.

At 2:30 p.m., the guns at Sumter were ready to present their final salute. As the garrison assembled on the parade ground, Lieutenant Hall took several gun crews to the parapet facing the ocean to fire the salute. The United States flag was raised for the last time. On Sullivan's Island, Beauregard was waiting impatiently with the previous landing party, including Pickens, for the ceremony to be completed so that they could enter Sumter.

Beauregard counted the gun salutes. Jut before the count of fifty shots, there was an explosion at the fort. One of the guns misfired, killing Private Daniel Hough and wounding the other members of the crew. Hough had a history of mental illness, and several officers in Anderson's command theorized that this was an act of suicide. Regardless, Hough was now the first man killed in this new war.

The ceremonies were stopped to tend to the wounded. Private Edward Gallway and Private George Fielding were transported to the hospital in Charleston. Gallway would die later that night. Three other wounded men were put aboard the *Isabel*. Hough was buried on the parade ground in the fort.

It was almost 4:30 p.m. when the garrison finally marched out of the fort to the tune of "Yankee Doodle." The musicians followed that song with "Hail to the Chief." With the long delay, the *Isabel* was now grounded on a shoal. Anderson and his men stayed onboard all night listening to the speeches in their fort and the great celebrations coming from the city. Anderson remarked to his officers, "God was pleased to guard my little force from the shell and shot into and against my work."

The Battery remained crowded with people. Boats all through the harbor displayed the Confederate flag. At dusk, The Citadel cadets held a dress parade on their drill field. That night, citizens were delighted to witness the crescent moon, reminiscent of the symbol on the Palmetto Flag.

Petigru was despondent over the events of the last several days. He wrote, "I felt for poor Anderson, deeply abandoned as he was to an obscure fate, to serve as a sort of stepping stone to a conflict in which he could reap no honor and left without a friend to stand by him and his followers while the fleet looked upon his distress with careless eyes." The next day, Petigru wrote to his sister:

> *That which was threatening a long time has come and the sword is drawn. It is an odd feeling to be in the midst of joy and gratulations that one does not feel. On the contrary it is a feeling of deep sadness that settles on my mind. The universal applause that waits on secessionists and secession has not the slightest tendency to shake my conviction that we are on the road to ruin. Nor could I entertain that the fiat of history will consign the actors in these scenes to the same lot with them who have ruined their country.*

That night, an ecstatic Governor Pickens gave an impassioned speech from the balcony of the Charleston Hotel:

The Union Is Dissolved!

We have defeated their twenty millions. We have humbled the flag of the United States before the Palmetto and Confederate, and so long as I have the honor to preside as your chief magistrate, so help me God, there is no power on earth shall ever lower from that fortress those flags, unless they be lowered and trailed in a sea of blood. I can here say to you it is the first time in the history of this country that the stars and stripes have been humbled. That flag has never before been lowered before any nation on this earth. But today it has been humbled and humbled before the glorious little State of South Carolina.

On April 15, the next morning, the high tide lifted the *Isabel* and the steamer finally transported Anderson and his troops to the waiting fleet. As the ship passed, Confederate soldiers on Morris Island tipped their hats and stood at attention to honor their foes. At the bar, outside the entrance to the harbor, Anderson and his men were transferred to the USS *Baltic.*

Onboard the *Baltic*, Anderson wrote his final report to the Honorable Simon Cameron, secretary of war:

Having defended Fort Sumter for thirty-four hours, until the quarters were entirely burned, the main gates destroyed by fire, the gorge walls seriously impaired, the magazine surrounded by flames, and its door closed from the effects of the heat, four barrels and three cartridges of powder only being available, and no provisions remaining but pork, I accepted the terms of General Beauregard (being the same offered by him on the 11th instant, prior to the commencement of hostilities) and marched out of the Fort on Sunday afternoon, the 14th instant, with colors flying and drums beating, bringing away company and private property, and saluting my flag with fifty guns.

Robert Anderson, Major, First Artillery

A reporter for the *Mercury* recorded the views inside Fort Sumter after the Federal troops left:

Every point and every object in the interior of the fort, to which the eye was turned, except the outer walls and easements, which are still strong, bore the impress of ruin…The walls of the internal structure—roofless, bare, bleak and perforated by shot and shell—hung in fragments, and seemed in instant readiness to totter down. Near the centre of the parade ground was the hurried grave of the one who had fallen from the recent casualty… And so it was that the garrison, compelled to yield the fortress, had at least

Charleston and Fort Sumter in the Civil War

After inspection of Fort Sumter following Anderson's withdrawal, the *Mercury* reported, "Every point and every object in the interior of the fort...bore the impress of ruin."

the satisfaction of leaving it in a condition calculated to inspire the least possible pleasure to its captors.

Several weeks later, Beauregard honored Confederate Secretary of War Walker by sending him an artifact of the battle: "I have the honor to send you...the flag which waived on Fort Moultrie during the bombardment of Fort Sumter, and was thrice cut by the enemy's balls. Being the first Confederate flag thus baptized, I have thought it worth sending to the War Department for preservation."

Weeks later, Lincoln confided to a friend, Orville Browning, about Fort Sumter. Browning wrote of the meeting, "He himself conceived the idea, and proposed sending supplies, without an attempt to reinforce giving notice of the fact to Governor Pickens of South Carolina. The plan succeeded. They attacked Sumter—it fell, and thus, did more service than it otherwise could."

EPILOGUE

After the longest siege of the Civil War, lasting nineteen months, the Confederacy evacuated Charleston on the evening of February 17, 1865. Union troops occupied the city the next day.

Leslie's correspondent W.T. Crane entered the city and observed:

> *The appearance baffles all description; scarcely a house remains intact; in some instances a dozen shell have entered the same building; its glass invariably shattered in almost every window; roofs are crushed and walls lean, crack, and gape at you as you silently and thoughtfully gaze upon them; grass is growing in the streets;...Crows scream around the ruins; broken bricks, timbers and debris of all kind are heaped around...Look at it now, and we see the blight of the touch of secession's fingers.*

The capture of Charleston, seen as the heartbeat of secession, was celebrated throughout the North. In March, Secretary of War Edwin M. Stanton issued an order regarding Fort Sumter, the victim of the first shot:

> *At the hour of noon, on the 14th day of April, 1865, Brevet Major-General Anderson will raise and plant upon the ruins of Fort Sumter, in Charleston harbor, the same United States flag which floated over the battlements of that fort during the rebel assault, and which was lowered and saluted by him, and the small force of his command, when the works were evacuated on the 14th of April, 1861.*

Anderson agreed to attend but his wife, an invalid, could not make the trip. Anderson traveled to Charleston by ship accompanied by his six-year-

The ceremony at Fort Sumter on April 14, 1865, once again raised the United States flag that had been retired by Major Anderson on his evacuation four years prior. *Courtesy of the Library of Congress.*

old son. Given the ruinous condition of accommodations in the city, he stayed on ship, as did most guests arriving for the ceremony.

On the morning of April 14, the harbor was crowded with vessels wanting to take part in the day's event. A large crowd, exceeding five thousand people, gathered at Fort Sumter. In attendance were Abner Doubleday and Norman Hall, who had served with Anderson in 1860–61.

Reverend Matthias Harris, the chaplain who had given the prayer on December 27, 1860, again opened the ceremony with a prayer. Anderson was accompanied by his faithful friend, police Sergeant Peter Hart. Hart had the garrison's mailbag containing the Fort Sumter flag that was lowered on April 14, 1861. He held the flag up for all to see, to the roars of the crowd.

Anderson stood to speak and, filled with emotion, stated:

> *I am here, my friends, my fellow-citizens and fellow-soldiers, to perform an act of duty to my country dear to my heart, and which all of you will appreciate and feel. Had I observed the wishes of my heart it should be done in silence; but in accordance with the request of the Honorable Secretary of War, I make a few remarks, as by his order, after four long, long years of war; I restore to its proper place this dear flag, which I floated here during peace before the first act of this cruel rebellion. I thank God that I lived to see this day, and to be here, to perform this, perhaps the last act of my life, of duty to my country. My heart is filled with gratitude to that God who has so singly blessed us, who has given us blessings beyond measure. May all the nations bless and praise the name of the Lord, and all the world proclaim, Glory to God in the highest, and on earth peace, good-will toward men.*

Anderson was so overwhelmed that he could not raise the flag alone. With the help of Hart and several sailors there, the old, tattered flag was raised to the top of the 150-foot-tall flagstaff.

The band played "The Star-Spangled Banner" as the crowd wept and hugged. Salutes were fired from each of the remaining Confederate batteries around the harbor. The guns of the Union fleet in the harbor were also fired in honor of the day.

At 6:00 p.m., a great banquet was given at the Charleston Hotel by the commanding general of now occupied Charleston. Many speeches and toasts were given during the three-hour dinner. The final toast of the evening was reserved for Anderson. After his introductory remarks, he raised his glass and offered:

> *I beg you now, that you will join me in drinking to the health of another man whom we all love to honor, the man who, when elected President of the United States, was compelled to reach the seat of government with an escort, but now could travel all over the country with millions of hands and hearts to sustain him. I give you the good, the great, the honest man, Abraham Lincoln.*

As everyone in the hall was joining in the toast, it was several minutes past 10:00 p.m. At that same moment, in Washington, D.C., at Ford's Theater, John Wilkes Booth fired the fateful shot at the head of the president.

BIBLIOGRAPHY

Adams, Charles. *When in the Course of Human Events: Arguing the Case for Southern Secession*. New York: Rowman & Littlefield Publishers, Inc., 2000.

Burton, E. Milby. *The Siege of Charleston: 1861–1865*. Columbia: University of South Carolina Press, 1970.

Carson, James Petigru. *Life, Letters and Speeches of James Louis Petigru, Union Man of South Carolina*. Washington, D.C.: W.H. Lowdermilk & Company, 1920.

Castel, Albert. *Fort Sumter: 1861*. Harrisburg, PA: Eastern Acorn Press, 1981.

Catton, Bruce. *The Coming Fury*. Garden City, NY: Doubleday & Company, 1961.

Charleston Courier. Charleston, SC, 1860–61.

Chesnut, Mary Boykin. *A Diary from Dixie*. Edited by Ben Amos Williams. Boston: Houghton Mifflin Company, 1949.

Cisco, Walter Brian. *Taking a Stand: Portraits from the Southern Secession Movement*. Shippensburg, PA: White Mane Books, 2000.

Crawford, Samuel W. *The Genesis of the Civil War: The Story of Sumter, 1860–1861*. New York: Charles L. Webster & Company, 1887.

Detzer, David. *Allegiance: Fort Sumter, Charleston and the Beginning of the Civil War*. New York: Harcourt, Inc., 2001.

Doubleday, Abner. *Reminiscences of Forts Sumter and Moultrie in 1860–61*. New York: Harper & Brothers, 1876.

Eaton, Clement. *A History of the Southern Confederacy*. New York: Free Press, 1954.

Frank Leslie's Illustrated Newspaper. New York, 1860–61.

Harper's Weekly Journal of Civilization. New York, 1860–61.

Heyward, DuBose, and Herbert R. Sass. *Fort Sumter, 1861–65*. New York: 1932.

Illustrated London News. London, England, 1860–61.

Klein, Maury. *Days of Defiance: Sumter, Secession and the Coming of the Civil War*. New York: Vintage Books, 1999.

Lawton, Eba Anderson. *Major Robert Anderson and Fort Sumter 1861*. New York: Knickerbocker Press, 1911.

Lebby, Dr. Robert. "The First Shot on Fort Sumter." *South Carolina Historical and Genealogical Magazine* (July 1911).

Mercury. Charleston, SC, 1860–61.

Minutes of the Washington Light Infantry, Charleston, SC.

Porter, A. Toomer, D.D. *Led On! Step by Step*. New York: G.P. Putnam and Sons, 1898.

Potter, David M. *The Impending Crisis, 1848–1861*. New York: Harper & Row, 1976.

Robertson, William H.P. *The History of Thoroughbred Racing in America*. New York: Bonanza Books, 1964.

Schreadley, R.L. *Valor and Virtue: The Washington Light Infantry in Peace and In War*. Spartanburg, SC: Reprint Publishers, 1997.

Sketch of the Racing Mare Albine. Columbia, SC: The State Company, 1913.

Snowden, Yates, LLD, ed. *History of South Carolina.* Chicago: Lewis Publishing Company, 1920.

Stokeley, Jim. *Fort Moultrie: Constant Defender.* Washington, D.C.: U.S. Department of Interior, 1985.

Storey, Graham. *The Letters of Charles Dickens.* Oxford: Clarendon Press, 1998.

Swanberg, W.A. *First Blood: The Story of Fort Sumter.* New York: Charles Scribner's Sons, 1957.

War of the Rebellion: A Compilation of the Official Records of the Union and Confederate Armies. Washington, D.C.: Government Printing Office, 1880–1901.